MARTIN LUTHER KING, JR. AND THE CIVIL RIGHTS MOVEMENT

Edited by David J. Garrow

A CARLSON PUBLISHING SERIES

Atlanta, Georgia, 1960-1961

SIT-INS AND STUDENT ACTIVISM

Edited with a Preface by David J. Garrow

CARLSON
Publishing Inc

BROOKLYN, NEW YORK, 1989

Library of Congress Cataloging-in Publication Data

Atlanta, Georgia, 1960-1961 : sit-ins and student activism / edited
  with a preface by David J. Garrow.
         p.   cm. — (Martin Luther King, Jr. and the Civil Rights
Movement ; 9)
    Bibliography: p.
    Includes index.
    1. Afro-Americans—Civil rights—Georgia—Atlanta—History—20th
century. 2. Civil rights demonstrations—Georgia—Atlanta–
–History—20th century. 3. College students—Georgia—Atlanta–
–Political activity—History—20th century. 4. Atlanta (Ga.)—Race
relations. I. Garrow, David J. 1953-   . II. Series.
F294.A89N418   1989
975.8'231043—dc20   89-15714
ISBN 0-926019-05-8 (alk. paper)

Typographic design: Julian Waters

Typeface: Bitstream ITC Galliard

The index to this book was created using NL Cindex, a scholarly indexing program
from the Newberry Library.

For a complete listing of the volumes in this series, please see the back of this book.

Printed on acid-free, 250-year-life paper.

Manufactured in the United States of America.

Contents

Series Editor's Preface vii

History of the Negro Upper Class in Atlanta, Georgia,
   1890-1958, by *August Meier & David Lewis* 3

The Functions of Disunity: Negro Leadership
   in a Southern City, by *Jack L. Walker* 17

Protest and Negotiation: A Case Study of Negro
   Leadership in Atlanta, by *Jack L. Walker* 31

Sit-Ins in Atlanta: A Study in the Negro
   Revolt, by *Jack L. Walker* 59

The Strategy of a Sit-In, by *C. Eric Lincoln* 95

A Stormy Rally in Atlanta, by *Lionel Newsom*
   & *William Gorden* 105

The Atlanta Sit-In Movement, 1960-1961,
   An Oral Study, by *Vincent D. Fort* 113

Appendix: *An Appeal For Human Rights* 183

Bibliographical Information and Acknowledgements 189

Index 191

Series Editor's Preface

More than any other single locale, Atlanta, Georgia, was the centerpiece city for the southern black freedom struggle of the 1950s and 1960s. Black Atlanta even in the early 1950s possessed a tradition of civic activism that only a few other southern black communities—such as Durham and Winston-Salem, North Carolina, and Tuskegee, Alabama—could then equal, and its roster of important black-owned businesses and professional institutions—particularly the Atlanta University Center colleges—was one that no other southern town or city could match. The offspring of that community, and the graduates of those colleges—Martin Luther King, Jr., being only one of many—played significant roles in innumerable cities and towns across the south. Those links helped make Atlanta the true crossroads of the black south, even more so than the ubiquitous jokes about the centrality of Atlanta to the region's travel routes—"you change in Atlanta"—themselves suggested.

In light of the undeniable importance of black Atlanta to both the black South of the '50s and '60s and to national American politics in the years since, it is quite surprising as well as regrettable that no major, comprehensive scholarly study of black Atlanta, either during the civil rights era and/or since that time, has yet been published. While valuable analyses of some important black communities, such as Robert J. Norrell's *Reaping the Whirlwind* on Tuskegee and William Chafe's *Civilities and Civil Rights* on Greensboro, North Carolina, have appeared in the course of the 1980s, the absence of similar studies of cities such as Atlanta and Birmingham, Alabama, is particularly glaring.

With regard to Atlanta, that absence of any comprehensive scholarly study is most starkly visible with regard to the years 1960 and 1961, when Atlanta, in partial conjunction with Nashville, Tennessee, served as the major birthplace for the black southern student movement that began with the lunch counter sit-ins in the spring of 1960 and culminated in the creation and emergence of SNCC, the Student Nonviolent Coordinating Committee, as the cutting-edge cadre of the burgeoning southern struggle. Major works on Dr. King and on SNCC, such as my own *Bearing the Cross* (1986) and Clayborne Carson's *In Struggle* (1981), treat some of the important 1960 and 1961 events in Atlanta, but not in the detail or length that they deserve.

The lack of any comprehensive scholarly study of black Atlanta in those crucial years does not mean, however, that there is a total absence—or anything close to it—of valuable scholarly analyses on the topic. Indeed, if one puts together—as is done in this volume—a combination of scholarly materials produced over nearly thirty years time, one can assemble an extremely strong collection that sheds important light on the political dynamics of black Atlanta both during and prior to those landmark years of 1960 and 1961.

For the pre-1960 period, August Meier and David Lewis's 1959 study of the "Negro Upper Class" for the first six decades of the twentieth century is a valuable beginning point for anyone seeking to understand "pre-movement" black Atlanta, and particularly that generation of black ministers and businessmen whom Martin Luther King, Sr., and attorney A. T. Walden have often symbolized. Business and professional men from oftentimes modest family backgrounds—e.g. King, Sr.—had by the 1950s built a solid roster of impressive black institutions and organizations, institutions that had allowed black Atlanta's civic elite to play a significant and growing role in the public affairs of what was still a very rigidly-segregated city.

For these economically-established black adults, entre and influence with white Atlanta's political and business leadership involved quiet and well-mannered behind-the-scenes contacts. For a younger generation of black Atlantans, and particularly for the young people who made up the student bodies of the Atlanta University Center colleges—Morehouse, Spelman, Clark and Morris Brown most significantly—ongoing acceptance of the strictures and humiliations of racial segregation required repudiation, not weary understanding. Stimulated by the February 1, 1960, onset of student lunch counter sit-ins in Greensboro, North Carolina, Atlanta's black college students began their own organizing efforts. Cautioned by their college presidents to move carefully, the students prepared an extensive written statement challenging segregation—*An Appeal for Human Rights*, published in each of Atlanta's newspapers—and held a generally unproductive meeting with Mayor William B. Hartsfield before actually beginning sit-in protests at segregated establishments on March 15. Over seventy participants were arrested, but low-key negotiations with white business owners slowly got underway as the student sit-ins continued. By late May, with no changes or resolution having occurred, the black adult establishment organized a committee to spur discussions between the students and the white business community, but a late June meeting of the students with prominent department store owner Richard H. Rich resulted in no segregationist concessions. The situation remained static throughout the summer, with modest picketing and sit-ins continuing into September and October. By mid-October, with no sign of any white concessions in the offing, the students decided that significantly intensified sit-ins should begin.

The student leadership successfully persuaded a reluctant Martin Luther King, Jr., to join in on the first day of the new effort, and King's arrest, coupled with those of thirty-five other protesters, brought heightened media attention to the Atlanta sit-ins. King's confinement generated expressions of concern from Democratic presidential candidate John F. Kennedy. Atlanta Mayor William B. Hartsfield, aided by the black adult leadership, persuaded the students to suspend all protests for thirty days in exchange for his efforts to persuade the white merchants to desegregate their store facilities. Although King soon obtained a highly-publicized release from ongoing imprisonment, Hartsfield's good faith efforts with the merchants achieved no success, and by the beginning of 1961 the situation remained unresolved, with ongoing small-scale student picketing and a growing concern among the white leadership that national news coverage of the story was harming the city's business reputation.

Working behind the scenes, elderly black attorney A. T. Walden and politically influential white lawyer Robert Troutman, Sr., in conjunction with Chamber of Commerce president Ivan Allen, Jr., brokered a biracial adult consensus that the downtown store facilities would be desegregated within thirty days of the initial desegregation of the city's public school system, expected to occur that coming September. The black adults persuaded the two principal student leaders to accept the delayed-schedule accord as well, but once word of the less-than-immediate resolution began to spread through black Atlanta, the student community expressed considerable anger and talked of repudiating the adults' accord.

Only the persuasive rhetoric of Martin Luther King, Jr., at a penultimate black community rally on March 10 at Warren Memorial Methodist Church saved the settlement and prevented an open generational breach between black Atlantans. The audience accepted King's powerful appeal that the community could not reject its leaders and their efforts, and the student protests were suspended. Early that next fall, on schedule, the downtown stores desegregated their facilities, some eighteen months after the onset of the Atlanta student movement.

Jack Walker's 1963 and 1964 analyses of the 1960-1961 student protests, and the political dynamics distinguishing the student efforts from those of their black elders, are extremely valuable works of scholarship. All three of his essays—his brief 1964 monograph as well as both of his 1963 journal articles—are united by the common theme that distinctly different political roles and approaches, such as those manifested by the students and the adults, can be equally valuable and necessary and can, in combination, prove more functional as a duo than either could by itself. While Walker's work may at times understate the generational tensions and competitiveness that separated the students from the established black adults, his work, much like Meier and Lewis's, which was based on some thirty oral history interviews, is tremendously strengthened and enriched by his reliance upon oral sources—thirty-six interviews conducted by Walker in Atlanta in April and May of 1962.

Two briefer pieces, both also quasi-contemporaneous, similarly offer valuable descriptions and insight into the Atlanta movement events of 1960 and 1961. C. Eric Lincoln's short article supplies relatively unique details about the organizational forms and responsibilities adopted by the Atlanta students, and Lionel Newsom and William Gorden's brief 1963 article supplies a truly invaluable account of the crucial March 10, 1961, community rally at which Dr. King, Jr., persuaded youthful black Atlanta not to reject the desegregation accord brokered by their elders.

Lastly, Vincent Fort's 1980 masters thesis offers a splendid and important portrait of the Atlanta student movement, especially for its earliest months in the spring of 1960. Like Meier & Lewis and Walker, Fort's work is heavily based upon oral history sources—some fifteen extended interviews in this case—and provides an excellent overview of the political dynamics of 1960 black Atlanta from the vantage point of twenty years distance in time. The Appendix reproduces for the first time since the original newspaper publication the students' *Appeal.*

All told, the accounts and analyses that are brought together in this volume provide as complete and comprehensive a description as is now possible of the crucial 1960-1961 events in Atlanta. Both in the works of acknowledged senior scholars such as Meier, Walker, and Lincoln, and in the work of much younger scholars such as Fort, this volume on Atlanta provides important works of scholarship that almost without exception have received less use and citation than ought to have been the case. Whether with regard to an important unpublished study such as Fort's, or with regard to significant but truly obscure pieces such as Newsom and Gorden's article and Walker's 1964 monograph, this volume offers a fuller scholarly picture of the 1960-1961 Atlanta protest movement than anything else presently available. I am very pleased that Carlson Publishing's eighteen volume series on *Martin Luther King, Jr., and the Civil Rights Movement* is able to bring all of these valuable studies to a wider audience, and I hope that this volume will play a significant role in helping stimulate the additional scholarly studies of black Atlanta—both in the early 1960s and since then—that are so historically necessary and richly deserved.

David J. Garrow

Atlanta, Georgia, 1960-1961

History of the Negro Upper Class in Atlanta, Georgia, 1890-1958

AUGUST MEIER & DAVID LEWIS

Down to the close of the nineteenth century the entrepreneurial class in the Negro community depended in considerable part upon the support of white customers. Though the range of occupations varied in different cities, this group was composed primarily of blacksmiths, tailors, barbers and other skilled artisans, hackmen and draymen, grocers and, less frequently, hotel owners, caterers, real estate dealers and contractors. Along with civil servants, teachers, pullman porters of good family background, domestic servants in the most elite white families, the more eminent and better educated ministers, a few doctors and an occasional lawyer, the more successful among these entrepreneurs formed the upper stratum in the Negro community during the late nineteenth century.[1]

By about 1900, however, significant economic and social changes were under way in the Negro community. A growing antipathy on the part of whites toward trading with Negro businessmen, and changes in technology and business organization, forced many of the small entrepreneurs out of business. At the same time the increasing urbanization of Negroes supplied a base for business dependent on the Negro market. Such businesses included banks (the first two founded in 1888), cemetery and realty associations, insurance enterprises, and numerous small retail and service establishments.

Of course certain businesses—such as newspapers, undertakers and some barbers and retail merchants—had always depended on the Negro market, and this group now increased in number. At the same time there appeared larger numbers of doctors and lawyers who, like the ministers and the great majority of teachers, served a segregated community. This shift in the economic base of the Negro bourgeoisie proceeded at an uneven pace, earlier and more rapidly in some cities than in others. Moreover, the process was relatively gradual, extending from the 1890's through the 1920's, by which time the newer enterprises were dominant.[2]

We were interested in ascertaining the extent to which this shift in the economic base of the Negro bourgeoisie had affected the class structure of the Negro community. To what extent had the older upper-class families of around 1900 survived (a) as an economic elite and (b) as a social elite? To what extent had individuals of a more obscure origin come to occupy a dominant place in the economic life of the Negro community, to what extent had they achieved upper-class status, and to what extent had they replaced the older upper-class families in status? It is our hypothesis that it was for the most part a newer rising group of men that formed the back-bone of the entrepreneurial group that depended on the Negro market, and that in time they and their families came to constitute not only the economic elite, but the social elite as well.

Very little research has been addressed to this problem. About the only relevant study is that of Drake and Cayton, who report that in Chicago during the 1920's the pre-World War elite, largely economically dependent on the white community, for the most part lost its status to a parvenu group, which, catering to the needs of the Negro community became the dominant figures in "Black Metropolis."[3]

The city of Atlanta was selected for this pilot study because of its importance as an industrial city of the New South. In view of the nature of the data most of our information was perforce obtained through interviews with residents who because of their social status, their length of residence in Atlanta, or their professional interests, would be expected to possess information relevant to this study. We interviewed about thirty people—social scientists on the faculties of the five schools comprising the Atlanta University Center (Atlanta and Clark Universities, Morehouse, Morris Brown and Spelman Colleges), prominent businessmen, professional people, descendants of old families, and women of high status. We asked our informants whom they considered upper-class at the turn of the century and whom they considered upper-class today; we sought information as to the changing criteria for upper-class status; and we attempted to secure as many complete family histories as possible of Atlanta families prominent in the past, the present, or in both periods. The important role of the social clubs in Atlanta society led us to pay special attention to their membership.

In view of its historical nature this study did not lend itself to the use of statistical techniques. Under the circumstances, and in view of the paucity of relevant historical documents, we felt that the data obtained by interviewing a variety of well-informed individuals, supplemented by information from such documentary sources as were available, would supply as close an approximation to the actual state of affairs as one is likely to get.

Among the Negro entrepreneurs in Atlanta in the 1890's, the druggist, most of the several grocers and the one or two undertakers appear to have had primarily a Negro clientele; but the shoemakers (including the city's leading one) and draymen served both races; the chief barber shops for whites were owned by Negroes; a rock contractor and at least one outstanding building contractor (both of whom employed both white and colored workers), and at least two realtors did business almost entirely with whites.[4] Of this group several of the grocers, barbers and draymen, one undertaker, the contractor and the realtors enjoyed upper-class status. Three doctors, a couple of politicians, at least one minister, probably one lawyer, in some instances the resident bishop of the African Methodist Episcopal Church, several postal employees and college teachers rounded out the membership of this group.[5] In contrast to cities like Augusta and Savannah, with their ante-bellum free aristocracies, the early elite in Atlanta came from the mostly mulatto house-servant group, who were in a few cases aided by whites with whom they maintained close relationships, but who ordinarily seized the advantages (as compared to the field hands) enjoyed by this group to pull themselves up by their own bootstraps.

Life for the mulatto aristocracy of old Atlanta (circa 1890-1910) centered primarily around the respectable First Congregational Church, select Atlanta University, and perhaps half a dozen exclusive social clubs. Many of the elite had themselves been educated at Congregationalist Atlanta University (or its affiliated grammar and secondary school) and ordinarily sent their children there to be prepared for teaching and other white collar occupations. However, a minority, connected with the A.M.E. Church, the Methodist church, North, and its affiliated Clark University, or with Atlanta Baptist (later Morehouse) College, were accorded recognition in the highest social

5

circles. The leading women's social club, for example, was founded by the daughter of an A.M.E. bishop. With but few exceptions all of these families lived in the then fashionable Auburn Avenue section of Northeast Atlanta. (Many of the families who now live on the West Side still refer nostalgically to "family homesteads" across town). Here they were set apart from the less fortunate groups, who were largely concentrated in Western Atlanta.[6]

The shift from a bourgeoisie with its economic roots largely in the white community, to one with its economic roots almost entirely in the Negro community, actually began during the period we have been describing. Prominent among these were the so-called "cooperative" insurance and real estate businesses. Negro leaders as early as 1890 founded the Georgia Real Estate Loan and Trust Company.[7] Illustrative of the trend were the activities of Alonzo F. Herndon, whose career encompasses the transition. Arriving at Atlanta a poor man, he established himself as the most prominent barber in the city, and then ventured into the rapidly expanding field of Negro insurance, founding the Atlanta Life Insurance Company in 1905[8] (today one of the leading Negro enterprises in the country). To cite another instance, at about the same time white discrimination against Negro customers led a graduate of Atlanta University to open a shoe store which race leaders urged Negroes to support.[9] Again, one family was wise enough during the time of the First World War to turn from a declining hack business and invest its capital in an undertaking establishment.

However, it is generally agreed that the chief stimulus to Negro business enterprise in Atlanta was the audacious vision of Hemon Perry, who arrived in the city in 1908. The son of a Texas grocer and farmer, Perry had received only a sixth or seventh grade education, but had been a successful cotton sampler and insurance agent in his native state. On the basis of his experience with such companies as the Equitable and the Manhattan Life, Perry in 1911 launched the Standard Life Insurance Company, the largest Negro enterprise of its time. During the next dozen years there appeared a series of subsidiary and related companies: a bank, the Citizens' Trust Company (1921), and a half dozen organizations intended to "serve" the needs of Negro consumers. These included the Service Company (a laundry and dry-cleaning establishment, 1917), the Service Pharmacies, the Service Realty Company, the Service Engineering and Construction Company, and the National Fuel Corporation (which owned coal mines in Tennessee).[10] In spite of glowing prospects the insurance company began encountering serious legal and financial difficulty by 1925 and failed a few years later.[11]

But Perry's failure was chiefly a personal one. For on the ruins of his empire a few energetic and better trained men who had worked under him established many of the most important businesses of present-day Atlanta. They include the reorganized Citizens' Trust Company (the only Negro bank belonging to the Federal Reserve System), the Yates and Milton Drug Stores, and the Mutual Federal Savings and Loan Association. Moreover, the opening up of the new fashionable West Side of Atlanta as a well-to-do residential area, grew out of the Perry Service Companies. Three of the most important businessmen in Atlanta today first entered Atlanta businesses through the Perry enterprises. Other businesses that have appeared in the last thirty-five to forty years have included a radio station, a cosmetic factory, a daily newspaper, another pharmacy, and—especially since the Second World War—a number of realty and contracting companies. All of these concerns depend upon the Negro market.[12]

It is noteworthy that the chief enterprises, save for the Atlanta Life Insurance Company, and the smaller of the two drug concerns, were created by men who were not members of the turn-of-the-century Atlanta elite. Even the majority of the directors of the Atlanta Life, though Congregationalists and graduates of Atlanta University, are from families who were not upper-class in Atlanta fifty years ago. The question then arises, to what extent has the economic dominance of this new elite affected the old social structure?

Considerable insight into the composition of the contemporary social elite is given by an examination of the social clubs. For purposes of analysis we have selected what Atlantans consider to be the two leading women's clubs and the two most prominent men's clubs. The former are "The Twelve," a social club, and the "Chautauqua Circle," a literary society composed of fifteen members. Both date back to about 1900. The town's leading men's clubs, both established in the 1920's, are the local "Boule" of the Sigma Pi Phi, a national business and professional fraternity, and the somewhat more recent "Twenty-Seven Club."

Approximately half of the original thirteen members of the Boule belonged to old elite families. Today, however, practically all of its nearly doubled membership are individuals whose families were not upper-class in Atlanta before the first World War.[13] The Twenty-Seven Club[14] is similarly composed for the most part of the newer business and professional men. The few members of these clubs who are descended from old elite Atlanta families are themselves prominent in the business life of present-day Atlanta. On the other hand economic and professional status is not the only criterion for membership in these clubs, for certain prominent and wealthy individuals either do not care to join or are excluded on the basis of personality characteristics.

Judging by the composition of these men's clubs (whose membership overlaps considerably), and judging also by the data supplied by our informants, the men who form the core of the upper-class in Atlanta today are the presidents of the six institutions of higher education, the leading businessmen (all of whom are connected with businesses based on the Negro market), some of the more distinguished physicians, a few professors who play strategic roles in the affairs of the Negro community, and a handful of other professional men. Of this group many are from respectable families, though only a few are from really prominent families at the apex of the social pyramid in Atlanta or elsewhere. On the other hand it would appear that only a few of them rose from lower-class background. On the fringes of this core group, and associating with its members to a considerable extent, are a number of college professors and professional and business men who do not rank with the highest elite socially, though comparable to its members in wealth or professional attainment or both. (Some parvenus are not really socially acceptable at all.) One can also find an occasional example of an individual who is a small businessman, but is rather well accepted socially because of his family background. Significantly, civil servants, who once comprised a considerable part of the elite, now tend to occupy a middle-status position. It is noteworthy, too, that grocers and undertakers no longer play the role that some entrepreneurs in those occupations once did, while the group of partisan-entrepreneurs who served the white community has quite disappeared.[15] It is thus apparent that the increasing economic differentiation of the Negro community has been reflected in the criteria for membership in the upper-class, though now as earlier college education is an important criterion of upper-class status, many of the most eminent businessmen in the city retaining close connections with the Atlanta schools either as alumni or professors in the business school. It should also be pointed out that due in large part to the fact that Atlanta University discontinued its undergraduate program over twenty-five years ago, the correlation between Atlanta University training and Congregational Church membership on the one hand, and social prominence on the other, has diminished.[16] Thus it is clear that only a handful of men who belong to the old elite families have a significant economic and social role in present-day Atlanta.

On the other hand, in contrast to the men's clubs, about half the members of the two leading ladies' clubs, the Chautauqua Circle and The Twelve, are members of the city's old elite families. With them must be classed a lady who came from a neighboring state about fifty years ago, but who became thoroughly identified with the old aristocracy and an important social arbiter. The other members of these two clubs owe their social prominence to the fact that they are married to men who have themselves achieved upper-class status in Atlanta during the last forty years. A few of this latter group come from distinctly elite families outside of Atlanta; the others have gained acceptance by virtue of the social power created by a combination of their husbands' standing and their own personalities. (There are cases of women whose husbands stand at or close to the top of Atlanta' social hierarchy, but are themselves unacceptable to the social arbiters among the women). Membership in both of these clubs, with their old-family leadership, is still a coveted honor; in part this is undoubtedly for the very reason that the club leaders have astutely admitted a judicious selection from the wives of Atlanta's new male elite. Moreover the influence of the old aristocratic families is not limited to these older clubs. For example, two other leading clubs, the Junior Matrons founded perhaps thirty years ago, and the recently established chapter of the new, nationwide Links, exhibit the same pattern of membership, with descendants of old families forming about half the membership.[17] That family background is still a significant criterion in upper-class status is indicated by the fact that many older members of these clubs, who are financially unable to move to the now fashionable West Side, are still regarded as among the social elite.

What has happened to the older elite families that no longer enjoy the highest status in Atlanta society? In the evidence made available to us, cases of marked downward social mobility are rare. It is, however, not uncommon to find people whose parents were at the top of the social hierarchy and who are themselves respectable and respected professional and business people, but who, unlike their parents, are on the fringe of the upper-class, are peripheral socially, rather than belonging to the most elite social groupings. Even more significant has been the large number—especially among the men—who have left Atlanta for other cities. The descendants of one socially very prominent grocer at the turn of the century have all left Atlanta, and several of them have become very prominent elsewhere. One exceedingly distinguished New York surgeon was also from an elite Atlanta family; in another case the descendant of a leading Atlanta physician is married to the president of a

9

noted medical school. These two, of course, have enjoyed upper-class status both in the cities of their birth and adoption.

In general then the data indicate that there has been a considerable elite circulation in Atlanta, though the continuing role of the older families, especially among the women, should not be minimized. There is, moreover, still something of a correlation between color and upper class status,[18] though this is not nearly so striking as it was half a century ago. On the other hand the fact that there appear to be so few extreme cases of downward mobility, and the fact that the disappearance of old families from Atlanta's upper-class is due largely to migration to other cities, suggests that to a considerable extent the situation might be described as a broadening of the base of the upper-class, rather than an actual substitution of new families for old families constituting that class. Moreover, as the upper-class has increased in size and as Atlanta Negroes have moved upward economically, greater social differentiation has taken place, so that many of those who today are what might be called "lower upper-class" though their parents were at the pinnacle of the social hierarchy, would have retained the highest status if the economic status of Negroes had remained unchanged, or if the upper-class population had remained smaller.

To what can one attribute the continued importance that Atlantans attach to the old families as evidenced by the continued importance of the older social clubs and the leadership that certain descendants of the old aristocracy exercise in social affairs in modern Atlanta? In part this is undoubtedly due to a natural lag between the shift in economic leadership and that in social leadership. However, it is our belief that the most important factor was undoubtedly the fortunate marriages made between certain daughters of the old families and some of the newer business and professional men—marriages that have tended, to a remarkable degree, to unite the descendants of the older aristocracy with the newer economic-social elite.

This tendency is revealed by several of the following family histories, which are illustrative of the developments described above:

One of the most distinguished families among Atlanta's old mulatto aristocracy was that of a man who came from a northwestern Georgia town to Atlanta University, and established his realty business about 1890. From then until his death about twenty years ago, his clientele was almost entirely white. His wife, whose forbears had been the house slaves of a distinguished Georgia planter family, became a member of the Chautauqua Circle. All of the children attended Atlanta University. Two of them became professional people and later left Atlanta; a third married a physician of some prominence in the new Atlanta, who came originally from central Georgia where his father had been the town's only ice-man. This couple's children have entered professional work and left town. Meanwhile, the wife carries on the family tradition of Chautauqua membership. And although she now resides on the fashionable West Side, she nostalgically recalls her pleasant childhood days in the old section of the city when, as she expressed it, "family and character were more important than they are today" as criteria of social acceptability.

Among the small circle of people with whom this lady associated as a youngster were the children of one of Georgia's two or three most distinguished Federal officeholders during the administrations of Presidents McKinley and Roosevelt. This man, who owned a Decatur Street barbershop frequented by white politicians, and who headed up the Georgia Real Estate Loan and Trust Company mentioned above, married the daughter of a Reconstruction congressman, and sent all of his children to Atlanta University. One of his daughters married the outstanding colored contractor in Atlanta in recent years, a new settler, but a man who has been consistently influential in the development of the West Side. Though preferring the solitude of their sprawling estate to the glitter of Atlanta's social life, this couple must be regarded as belonging to the city's upper crust.

Of the three leading men formerly connected with the Hemon Perry enterprises, none of whom were natives of Atlanta, two have married into old elite families. One of them was descended from residents of a midwestern Northern city since before the Civil War, where one grandfather was in the dray business and the other one a barber. Coming to Atlanta University from a neighboring state where his father was a retail businessman with both Negro and white customers, he became connected with Perry and married a descendant of one of the most prominent white families of antebellum Atlanta. Both his wife and her parents were also graduates of Atlanta University, and her father was a Congregationalist minister from Savannah. Her mother founded a noted charity which the daughter now directs, and was a charter member of the Chautauqua and The Twelve. The daughter, active in both groups, is widely regarded as the chief social arbiter among Atlanta ladies. When she and her husband built a West Side home in the middle twenties, it heralded the exodus of Atlanta's elite from the Auburn Avenue section.[19]

Another of Atlanta's leading businessmen, son of a border-city high school teacher and graduate of a famous Northern university, was certainly far from wealthy when he married the Atlanta University-educated granddaughter of two of Atlanta's old elite businessmen—one an undertaker, and the other a grocer with white customers. The undertaker, born a slave, like many others of the late nineteenth century mulatto elite had migrated to Atlanta from a smaller Georgia town. With only the most informal of educational backgrounds he worked as a railroad porter, acquired some land, and entered the undertaking business around 1880. Quite unusual for a family that belonged to the elite, his family belonged to the A.M.E. Church, though the children went to Atlanta University. While the family as a group must still be counted among Atlanta' upper stratum, the granddaughter who married the successful businessman from the border states was the one selected by the Chautauqua to carry on the family membership, and her marriage in time certainly enhanced her own and her family's position. Her husband's grandparents were on one side trusted house slaves, and on the other side of free ancestry. After the Civil War one grandparent was a chef at a prominent hotel, the other a doorman for an important government official—both coveted jobs at the time. His father's professional training and occupation as teacher illustrate the rising educational attainments of the late nineteenth century Negro bourgeoisie; the distinguished Atlanta businessman himself illustrates the continuing mobility of his family.

Not generally regarded as in the very highest circles, but still representative of the mulatto elite was the family of a lady who ran a hack stand during the late nineteenth and early twentieth centuries, while her husband was a shoemaker and grocer. Both of their businesses and their home were near Atlanta University on the western side of town rather than in the Auburn Avenue Section. After her husband's death, and before the hacking business had petered out—as it was doing by the time of the First World War—she and her sons shrewdly established an undertaking business that is still run by one of her daughters-in-law. Several of her children left the city, but one of them married a man who for about ten years around 1900 ran the only restaurant for whites in a noted antebellum town. Of the six children of this union, all but one daughter (who was graduated from Clark) finished at Atlanta University. The son became an elementary school principal. Four daughters left the city, two of them, as many Atlantans say, "marrying up" into the family of a very eminent grocer, all of whose descendants, however, have also left the city, and are leading distinguished lives elsewhere. The fifth daughter married a postal employee and obtained a home in Northeast Atlanta shortly before the move to the West Side began; this lady carries on her mother's club membership in the Inquirers, an old and distinguished literary club, although somewhat below the Chautauqua in the social hierarchy.

Rather rare are the descendants of the old elite who have maintained or increased their wealth without marrying into newer families. Yet even today few families could rank in status with the descendants of a postal employee and important official in the Congregational Church half a century ago, who was an alumnus of Atlanta University. His wife belonged to both the Chautauqua Circle and The Twelve. Their children went to Atlanta University and entered the professions, the youngest becoming a noted race leader nationally. Of the two daughters who remained in Atlanta, one married the Atlanta University trained son of a respectable postal employee and Congregationalist, who unlike others did not leave the city to seek his fortune, but became a leading figure in the business community. He was thus one of the few sons of old families who acquired a prominent place in the business life of present-day Atlanta, thus perpetuating and perhaps improving his family's position among the economic and social elite. His wife of course carries on her mother's affiliation with the Chautauqua and The Twelve.

The findings of this study then indicate that economic leadership in the Atlanta Negro community has very largely passed into the hands of a group of professional and businessmen who have come to Atlanta or risen to prominence there in the past thirty-five years, and that connected with the shift in economic power there has been a related change in the composition of the upper class, with the very highest social status being accorded to certain men prominent in business and professional life today, even though most of them are not of distinguished old Atlanta families. The few male descendants of the old social and economic elite who are recognized as important social leaders today are those who have successfully made their place in the new economic world whose chief enterprises are the Atlanta Life Insurance Company, the Citizens' Trust Company, and the Mutual Federal Savings and Loan Association. Among women on the other hand, a high proportion of descendants of the old families still retain the highest social status. This is especially true of those who have married the founders of the newer fortunes, and their social connections with other old families (especially through the women's clubs) have served to bolster the prestige of the older aristocracy. Though considerably diminished, the social role of descendants of the old aristocracy is still significant. It is possible that the displacement of the older upper class has been less complete in southern cities than in northern cities, if the findings of Drake and Cayton in regard to Chicago are representative. Future studies should be conducted therefore to ascertain to what extent this pattern has been followed in other cities North and South.

[Part of the research for this article was done under a research grant from Morgan State College.]

Notes

1. On the role of Negro business and businessmen in the late nineteenth century see W.E.B. DuBois, *The Philadelphia Negro* (Philadelphia, 1898), 115-31; Jeffrey R. Brackett, *The Colored People of Maryland Since the War* (Baltimore, 1890), 28-29, 37-39; DuBois, ed., *The Negro in Business* (Atlanta University Publications No. 4, 1899) *passim*: St. Clair Drake and Horace Cayton, *Black Metropolis* (New York, 1945), 433-34; *Christian Educator V*, (July 1894), 167-68; *Proceedings of the National Negro Business League*, 1900 (no imprint, 1900) *passim*: Robert A. Warner, *New Haven Negroes: A Social History* (New Haven, 1940), 233; DuBois, "The Negroes of Farmville, Virginia: A Social Study," *Bulletin of the Department of Labor* No. 14 (1898), 17-19, 20; DuBois, "The Negro in the Black Belt: Some Social Sketches," *Bulletin of the Department of Labor*, No. 22 (1899, pp. 403, 407, 408, 412, 413, 415; Abram L. Harris, *The Negro as Capitalist* (Philadelphia, 1936), chaps. iii-viii.

2. Harris, *Ibid.*; Joseph Pierce, *Negro Business and Business Education* (N.Y., 1947), chap. i; Drake & Cayton, *Black Metropolis,* 434-37; DuBois, ed. *Some Efforts of Negroes for Their Own Social Betterment* (Atlanta University Publications No. 3, 1898), 18-27; DuBois, *Economic Co-Operation Among Negro Americans* (Atlanta University Publications No. 12, 1907), *passim*; Mary White Ovington, *Half a Man* (N.Y., 1911), chap. V; George Edmund Haynes, *The Negro at Work in New York City* (N.Y., 1912), Part II; R.R. Wright, Jr., "The Negro in Philadelphia," *A.M.E. Church Review*, XXIV (July 1907), 137-39; R. Wright, *The Negro in Pennsylvania* (Philadelphia, [1909]), 30-33; Booker T. Washington, "Durham, North Carolina; A City of Negro Enterprise," *Independent*, LXX (1911), 542-50; E. Franklin Frazier, "Durham: Capital of the Black Middle Class," in Alain Locke, ed., *The New Negro* (New York, 1925), 333-40; Ray Stannard Baker, *Following the Color Line* (New York, 1908), 39-44; Warner, *New Haven Negroes*, 233-36; DuBois, "The Economic Revolution in the South," in Washington and DuBois, *The Negro in the South* (New York, 1907), 95-101; Annual *Reports* of the National Negro

Business League (imprint varies), 1900 et seq.; Ira De A. Reid, *The Negro in the American Economic System* (memorandum for the Carnegie-Myrdal Study of the Negro in America, 1940), 3 vols.; E. Franklin Frazier, *Negro Youth at the Crossways* (Washington, 1940) *passim*; DuBois, *Philadelphia Negro, loc. cit.;* John Daniels, *In Freedom's Birthplace* (Boston, 1914), 362-73.

3. Drake and Cayton, *Black Metropolis*, 543-44. Unfortunately, E. Franklin Frazier's provocative *Black Bourgeoisie* (Glencoe, Ill., 1957), does not deal with how the historical development of the class structure was related to the economic process we have described. John Daniels in his study of Boston Negroes just prior to World War I, described an upper class economically and socially allied with the white community, and a rising middle class many of whose members were entrepreneurs serving the Negro community. (*In Freedom's Birthplace*, 174-85).

4. For partial accounts of Negro business in Atlanta in 1890's see Clarence A. Bacote, "The Negro in Georgia Politics, 1880-1908." (Unpublished doctoral dissertation, University of Chicago, 1955) 5-7 (Bacote also mentions a Negro dentist who had white customers at least as late as 1890); E. R. Carter, *The Black Side*, (Atlanta, 1896) *passim*; Robert J. Alexander, "Negro Business in Atlanta," *Southern Economic Journal*, XVII (1951), 452-54. for partial account of Atlanta business about 1907 see R. Baker, *Following the Color Line*, 38-44.

5. Interestingly enough men of the cloth, though important in the affairs of the Negro community, do not usually appear to have attained the highest social status. This situation was related to the fact that the bulk of the clergy belonged to denominations such as the Baptist, A.M.E. and A.M.E. Zion, rather than the elite churches.

6. At that time only three of the schools—Atlanta University, Atlanta Baptist College, and Spelman Seminary (now college) were located on the West Side. For descriptions of slums near these schools see Ridgely Torrence, *Story of John Hope* (New York, 1948), 139.

7. Bacote, "Negro in Georgia Politics," 6.

8. For brief discussion of Herndon see Baker, *Following the Color Line*. 43.

9. *Ibid.*, 39-40.

10. These concerns constituted a small interlocking empire. Funds of the insurance company formed the chief deposits of the bank; the bank in turn could finance the operations of the service companies; the construction company built the houses on the lands sold by the realty company, whose sales were made possible by mortgage loans made by Standard Life, whose chief investments were in unimproved lands on the West Side of Atlanta.

11. A useful compendium of materials on Perry is available in C. L. Henton, ed., "Hemon E. Perry: Documentary Materials for the Life History of a Business Man," (Master's Thesis, Atlanta University, 1948). Perry left the city and died soon after.

12. For some material on the recent economic developments in Atlanta see Emmet John Hughes, "The Negro's New Economic Life," *Fortune*, LIV (Sept., 1956), 248, 250. For material on condition sin the late 1940's see Alexander, "Negro Business in Atlanta," 455-61.

13. For roster of original and 1952 members of Atlanta Boule see Charles H. Wesley, *History of the Sigma Pi Phi* (Washington, 1954), 361-62.
14. In addition to its social functions, the Twenty-Seven Club functions in the political power structure of the city. Negroes in Atlanta in fact exercise unusual political power for a southern city, and their votes are generally credited with the recent re-elections of Mayor Hartsfield. (See Douglass Cater, "Atlanta: Smart Politics and Good Race Relations," *The Reporter*, July 11, 1957, esp. p. 19) One informant, however, insisted that the belief which Negroes hold as to their role in the political power structure of the city is mostly myth.
15. The pattern of exclusion of ministers from elite circles noted above continues. Perhaps half a dozen clergymen may be said to occupy positions in the core of the upper class; of these four are college presidents, and it is to be presumed that their social positions are attributable to this fact. That power and social status may be quite distinct is illustrated by the fact that the minister who probably has the most power in the Negro community, by virtue of his influence with the masses, is not considered upper class; the same is true of a leading and respected fraternal figure. Nor is the N.A.A.C.P presidency held by a member of the upper class.
16. To some extent Morehouse College has taken over Atlanta University's role as a road to economic and social status for young men.
17. This discussion of social clubs is based on interview material and lists of club members. In a perceptive study of a sampling of voluntary associations in Atlanta, Lois E. Johnson, utilizing a modified form of Warner's Index of Status Characteristics, places both the Chautauqua Circle and the Twenty-Seven Club at the pinnacle of Atlanta society, with a membership upper and upper-middle class in terms of its economic and educational attainments. (Miss Johnson did not include The Twelve and the Boule in her study.) See Lois E. Johnson, "Voluntary Associations: A Study in Status Behavior," Master's Thesis, Atlanta University, 1952, esp. p. 24.)
18. Though it is widely held that skin color is no longer a criterion of social status among Negroes, the statement of those informants who discussed the matter—with one exception—and such observations as were ourselves made support the view that there still exists *some correlation* between social class and skin color in Atlanta, especially among the women.
19. Census tract data and Block Statistics derived from the 1950 census support the information derived from informants as to the residential distribution of the upper class. For example the homes with the highest assessment are located in certain blocks of tract 29 in the older Northeast area, and in certain West Side tracts, especially tracts 24 and 40. See U.S. Bureau of the Census, *U.S. Census of Population*, 1950, Vol. III, *Census Tract Statistics*, chap. ii (Washington, 1952); and *Ibid.*, Vol. V. *Block Statistics*, part 9 (Washington, 1952). Since 1950 the movement to the West Side has continued, and the residential area for middle and upper class Negroes has expanded considerably.

The Functions of Disunity:
Negro Leadership in A Southern City

JACK L. WALKER

Introduction

During the last five years waves of Negro protest demonstrations have swept across the Southern states. Incidents like the Montgomery bus boycott, the freedom rides and the sit-ins have spread with amazing speed, provoking racial crises in numerous towns and cities, even in the Deep South, and often taking the white leaders by surprise. From these crises a new type of Negro leadership seems to be arising: one dedicated to protest rather than accommodation and determined to press its demands for equality with a wide range of weapons including economic boycotts, civil disobedience, and political reprisals, tactics that Southern Negroes have never used in the past.

As the new, more militant leaders have arisen in Negro communities, the established leadership has usually offered resistance, and as a result many Southern Negro communities have been torn by disunity and internal conflict. Lewis M. Killian and Charles U. Smith in investigating Tallahassee, Florida, following a sharp dispute over bus segregation in the city found that the more militant, "protest" leaders had completely displaced the established Negro leadership. They found that after the crisis had passed, not one of the six persons named by a panel of both whites and Negroes as the top Negro leaders before the dispute were included as top leaders after the dispute. Also, not one of the five persons that the panel named as top Negro leaders after the dispute had been ranked among the first ten before the dispute took place. Even the old established leaders seemed to be aware that they had been displaced, and the study also indicated that a majority of the Negro community had shifted their allegiances to the protest leaders. Killian and Smith argue that:

> . . . the new leaders are becoming permanent leaders not because of the attractiveness of their personalities or their skill at organizing, but rather because they adhere rigorously to the *form* of militant leadership which is becoming the trend for Negroes throughout the United States.[2]

The situation in Tallahassee, however, does not seem to have been duplicated in all other Southern cities, or even in all those that have experienced a racial crisis within the last five years. Leslie Dunbar in commenting on the findings of Killian And Smith has argued that:

> There is some evidence in the stories of how a number of Southern cities have desegregated lunch counters to suggest that the older Negro leadership and the protest leaders can and do fruitfully complement each other, though coordination and mutual trust have sometimes been hard come by. My guess would be that this is the true interpretation. Negro leadership in the South is being broadened by an infusion of new elites.[3]

The subject of this essay is the relations between the established Negro leadership and the new protest leaders in a Southern city, the issue raised by Dunbar, Killian and Smith. The analysis is based on a case study of the sit-in controversy in Atlanta, Georgia, and is concerned particularly with the social and economic factors associated with the leaders' differing attitudes towards goals and techniques of social action. It will be argued that both the conservative and the protest leaders can play an important part in such racial disputes and unless the conservatives are completely displaced by the protest leaders, disputes among the leadership tend to increase, not decrease the effectiveness of the Negro community's battle against the institutions of segregation.

Sit-Ins in Atlanta: A Case Study[4]

On February 1, 1960, several Negro students sat down at a lunch counter in Greensboro, North Carolina, and refused to leave when told that the store did not serve Negroes. The manager is reported to have said: "They can just sit there. It's nothing to me." But within a week similar groups were sitting down in protest all over the South, and a major social movement was underway. The sit-ins spread even into the Deep South, and in response to fears and rumors that sit-ins were being planned the Georgia legislature passed a special trespass law on February 17, 1960.

Their fears were well founded, for as early as February 4 students at Atlanta University were planning demonstrations, but they were persuaded by faculty members and an apprehensive administration to postpone their action until they had drawn up a statement of their grievances. This statement was quickly completed and printed in the form of a full page advertisement in all local newspapers on March 9, 1960, under the title: "An Appeal for Human Rights." The advertisement caused a sensation in the state and it was commented on by politicians and public figures all over the country. This was followed on March 15 by the first wide spread sit-in demonstrations in Atlanta in which seventy-seven students were arrested under the new Georgia trespass law.

While their cases were pending in court the students began to work on several other projects. They mounted picket lines against food stores which had large Negro clienteles yet did not hire Negroes above the menial level, they had a series of meetings in Negro churches explaining the student movement and asking for support, they began publishing a weekly news sheet that eventually became a full fledged weekly newspaper, and on May 17, 1960, they gathered 1,400 students together to march on the State Capitol in downtown Atlanta to celebrate the Supreme Court's 1954 anti-segregation decision. This march was diverted by Atlanta's Chief of Police to prevent the students from meeting a large, ugly crowd that had gathered at the capitol. When the students left for summer vacation, tension was running high in the city.

During the Spring of 1960 there was considerable dispute among adult Negroes about the student movement. Although there were few who spoke out directly against the students, there were those who expressed their disapproval by keeping silent or withholding praise. The conservative adults, many of whom were businessmen, were opposed on principle to the

19

student's use of picket lines and boycotts against businesses which practiced discrimination in hiring. They were also apprehensive when they understood that the students were not satisfied with their first sit-ins and their march on the State Capitol, but were planning repeated demonstrations in an effort to force the issues. The adult community began to divide on their support for the students and rumors that all the Negro adults did not approve of the students' efforts passed through the white community.

Regardless of the criticism, the leaders of the student movement continued organizational and propaganda work during the summer. On June 27 they met privately with the president of the city's leading department store who tried to convince them to give up their demonstrations, promising that he would consider their grievances later on after the schools had been safely desegregated. This meeting broke down into a heated argument in which the student leaders are reported to have threatened the merchant with a boycott and the merchant shouted: "I don't need Negro trade!"

Following this incident conservative Negroes came into the open with criticisms of the students, and a few even made public speeches attacking their methods. But even so, after the students had returned for the fall term, on October 19, 1960, widespread sit-ins were mounted once again, and once again large numbers of demonstrators were arrested.[5] The students refused to leave the jail on bail at this time. Once again tension built up in the city. At this point the mayor asked for, and was granted, a thirty-day truce period in which he promised to try to reach a settlement of the dispute.

The mayor's efforts were completely unsuccessful. The leading merchants were in no mood to compromise with the demonstrators and were suspicious of the mayor who was quite anxious to get a settlement and whose political power rested firmly on Negro support. When the mayor called a meeting of the downtown merchants in his office, only the small ones attended who depended heavily on Negro trade and feared a boycott.

On their own the leading merchants decided to try informal methods to bring an end to the disturbances. The conservative leaders of the Negro community, those who had criticized the students during the summer and who had been considered the "spokesmen" of the Negro community in the past, were asked to attend a private meeting with the merchants. The meeting was secret but it seems that the Negroes were being asked to use their influence to persuade the demonstrators to cease their efforts and to wait until after the schools were desegregated to discuss the issue of lunch counter desegregation. After meeting twice they decided to invite one adult

Negro leader who had been a close advisor to the students, and the most influential student leader to a secret meeting in the Negro section of town so that the white merchants could offer their proposals. When these two men were contacted, however, they immediately became suspicious of the proceedings and decided to expose them. They made a public announcement that they were not a party to these secret negotiations, and when the conservative Negroes and the whites arrived at the meeting place television cameras were already set up and reporters were everywhere clamoring for statements.

After this incident, on November 25, 1960, the students resumed their sit-ins and also organized a full scale boycott of the downtown shopping area. A stalemate continued throughout the months of December and January, during which most of the lunch counters remained closed and the boycott of the downtown stores remained in effect.

Throughout this three month period of stalemate the students, equipped with short wave radios, had been sitting-in at lunch counters all over the city without incident. Either they had been ignored, or the counters had been closed, but on February 7, 1961, one restaurant manager in a federal office building invoked the trespass law and had the demonstrators arrested. During the next three days arrests continued daily with the students refusing once again to come out on bail. A protest march and rally was planned to take place in front of the jail on February 19, and it was feared that such a demonstration might result in a riot.

At this tense moment the student leaders themselves turned to one of the oldest, most respected Negro leaders and asked him to try to get negotiations started again. This man had made public statements backing the students at the beginning of the movement, but he was also widely considered to be a conservative and had attended the secret meetings with the white merchants in November, 1960. At this juncture, however, by utilizing friendships he had with influential white leaders, he was able to get negotiations started which eventually led to a settlement of the controversy. The agreement was announced on March 7, 1961. It called for desegregation of the lunch counters after the school desegregation had been completed during the fall of 1961, and, except for the firm agreement that the counters would be desegregated, it was essentially what the merchants had pressed for from the beginning. The actual desegregation took place on September 27, 1961.

The Functions Of Disunity

The sit-in controversy in Atlanta took place in a community which is still basically segregated. Although a few of the barriers have been broken down during the past five years there are still almost no social contacts between the leadership of the two racial groups and residential segregation places their homes far apart. This isolation of the leadership of the two communities from each other is a potentially disruptive element in the social structure of the city. If a crisis arises involving the crucial issue of race, communication between the leaders of the two racial groups, which is normally tenuous and rather formal, becomes very hard to maintain, and it is even more difficult to establish the circumstances in which negotiation of the difficulties that caused the crisis can take place.

During the controversy over the sit-in demonstrations in Atlanta such a breakdown in communications between whites and Negroes occurred, and at the same time relations among the Negro leaders were strained because of their disagreements over tactics. The conservative Negro leaders are primarily older businessmen, although there are also social workers, college administrators and ministers in this group. The more liberal group is made up of students, members of the staffs of various Negro improvement groups, college teachers, younger businessmen and ministers.[6]

The dispute within the Negro community revolves around the use of protest demonstrations and economic boycotts to press the attack on segregation. The conservatives never questioned, throughout the sit-in controversy in Atlanta, the goals of the students, and even when they agreed to attend secret meetings with the merchants they never failed to inform the whites that they thought the students' demands were justified, even if they did not approve of their methods.[7] The conservatives oppose boycotts and protest demonstrations primarily because they feel these public displays of discontent cause bitterness and rancor and tend to destroy the cordial, settled atmosphere which they feel is a necessary precondition to effective negotiations. They also fear economic retaliation more than the protest leaders, not only because of their own businesses, but also because they have worked hard to build institutions such as the Y.M.C.A., the Urban League, and many churches which depend heavily on contributions from influential whites. During the boycott that accompanied the sit-in affair in Atlanta some of these organizations began to lose white contributors as tension mounted. To some extent the conservative leaders have each made adjustments to the traditional position of the Negro in Southern society. Although none seems completely satisfied, in varying measures they have given up efforts to penetrate the dominant white society and consequently they have a greater commitment to the institutions within the Negro community.

The businessmen among the conservatives have frequent dealings with influential whites in the city; both the bank and savings and loan association operated by Negroes in Atlanta have very sizeable deposits from white customers. In fact, to a large extent, the power of the conservatives depends on their influence with the white community. They are spokesmen for the Negro community primarily because they have gained white recognition and favor, although their own achievements placed them in a position to be chosen for this role. Because of this process of selection, the protest leaders regard the conservatives with almost the same hostility they have for the whites, if not more so. They complain that the conservatives' power is based essentially on the Negro's fear of the power of the white man. They think that the established leaders have profited from the injustices of segregation by trading their human dignity for the opportunity to represent the whites within the Negro community.

The protest leaders are not so directly engaged in activities and institutions that serve the whole community as are the conservatives, and they deal more exclusively with the Negro community than the conservatives. Yet even so they do not feel as much committed to its maintenance; in fact they hate all that it stands for. Their work brings them into closer contact with the social, economic and political deprivations suffered by the Negro, and they tend to concentrate on these injustices and have fewer reasons to try to protect institutions, both charitable and commercial, that presently exist in the Negro community. They are under less compulsion than the conservatives to act with restraint or to compromise their demands in order to make limited material gains or to promote the fortunes of Negro businessmen. In this sense they stand outside the economic and social life of the established community and they try to keep the dominant leaders, both white and colored, at arm's length, guarding against being too friendly with politicians and certainly never asking them for favors or help of any kind. They try to conduct their affairs strictly on the basis of their moral principles, and for these reasons conservatives frequently regard them as "irresponsible" and find their attitudes toward politics and community leaders "unrealistic" or "hateful." One conservative leader in Atlanta, who has a reputation as a good tactician and organizer, acknowledged the importance of the student protest in bringing "more integration in less than two years than we gained in ten," but he also argued that "they will never get anything done on their own because they are cut off; they work in a righteous vacuum over there."

The protest leaders and the conservatives manifest considerable suspicion for each other, and in Atlanta a complete breakdown in relations between them is prevented primarily by the existence of several influential men who stand between these two groups and are not so deeply committed to either political style, or who are caught in ambiguous circumstances that prompt them to maintain contact with both protest and conservative leaders. These men tend to bind the Negro community together by providing lines of communication between leaders of all persuasions.

Even though the conservative and protest leaders distrust each other, during the Atlanta sit-in controversy at least, their efforts were complementary. In fact, if the Negro community is conceived of as a system designed to fight the institutions of segregation each of these groups performed a function in this situation. The students and the adult protest leaders, by organizing demonstrations and economic boycotts, created a crisis which had to be resolved, even if in doing so they raised the level of tension between the two racial groups in the city and caused a rather dangerous breakdown of communications. But the leaders of the protests did not have the power to resolve the crisis they had created because they had no basis for contact with the dominant white leaders. As James Q. Wilson suggests, one of the inherent difficulties of protest action is "that the discretion of the protest leader to bargain after he has acquired the resources with which to bargain is severely limited by the means he was forced to employ in order to create those resources."[8] From the beginning of the dispute the leading merchants refused to negotiate directly with the demonstrators whom they considered to be irresponsible troublemakers. In fact, the tactics pursued by the protest leaders were almost certain to antagonize the dominant whites. As Killian and Smith point out in describing the political style of the protest leaders:

> This new leadership is not of the accommodating type. it seeks gains for the Negro community through formal demands and requests, boycotts, lawsuits and voting. The protest leaders are not concerned with whether or not the whites high within the power structure know, like or want to deal with them.[9]

The more conservatively inclined leaders, utilizing their reputations and the connections they had built up with the white community through the years, had the function of resolving the crisis situation created by the protest leaders. In this case even the antagonism between the two groups was functional because it made the conservatives seem more reliable and responsible in the eyes of the whites, and so they were still able to act as negotiators when both sides were ready to compromise.

Those leaders in the middle, who did not identify completely with either the conservative or the protest leaders, had the function of moderating this conflict over tactics. Some individuals find themselves in this situation because they are subject to cross-pressures which restrain them from becoming attached to either side in the controversy. Others are not committed because they have a flexible attitude toward social action which prompts them to regard all tactical weapons as potentially useful. Regardless of the influences that put them in this position, however, these leaders in the middle provide both formal and informal links between the conservative and protest leaders.

The situation in Atlanta does not seem to have been unique. Something of this same kind of unanticipated cooperation and sharing of functions between protest and conservative Negro leaders seems to have taken place during the sit-in controversy in Knoxville, Tennessee. Negotiation began initially there without any demonstrations but broke down after four tedious months of talks. Sit-ins began on June 9, 1960, and a boycott was started five days later on June 14th. Merrill Proudfoot describes a meeting of the executive committee of the protest movement which took place on July 2, 1960, after about three weeks of demonstrations. The meeting was attended by the president of Knoxville College, who had not been involved in planning or staging the demonstrations, and he revealed that he had been contacted by an official of the Knoxville Chamber of Commerce who informed him that there was a movement underway to reopen negotiations. Proudfoot rather indignantly comments:

> The circuitous means of communicating with one another has lent a comic-opera aspect to the way this major community problem has been handled. It would seem sensible for one of the merchants to have called Crutcher or James [the leaders of the demonstrations] and said, "come on down and let's talk!" Instead the merchants hint to the Chamber of Commerce official that they might be willing; he contacts not Crutcher or James, but Colston—the one person in the Negro community who has the greatest status . . . and he in turn makes the contact within the Negro community."[10]

Also when a negotiating team was formed to formulate the final agreement to desegregate, Colston was included once again, but this time he was accompanied by Crutcher. Although the description is not so complete it seems that a similar process operated at Winston-Salem, North Carolina, where the agreement to desegregate the lunch counters was not formulated by the protest leaders. Clarence H. Patrick reports that:

> The demonstrators several times sought unsuccessfully for someone to organize and mediate a meeting between them and the store managers in an attempt to resolve the anti-segregation movement on the basis of some mutual agreement. The leaders of the protest never met, as a group, with the managers of the stores where the protest occurred.[11]

Conclusion

The evidence presented here suggests that not all Southern Negro communities have experienced the same changes in leadership that Killian and Smith detected in Tallahassee. In some cases it seems that a kind of tactical balance exists with both conservative and protest leaders playing a part in the fight for equality. However, there is no evidence that the period of change and transition in Negro leadership in Atlanta has ended. In fact, a major unsettling force seems to be developing beneath the level of leadership. Almost all the leaders interviewed, including the conservatives, felt that expectations are rising perceptibly throughout the Negro community as a result of recent successful attacks on the institutions of segregation. The Negro masses, who have traditionally been apathetic toward politics and efforts to fight segregation, seem to be gaining hope that change is possible and are shaking off the mood of cynical resignation that has paralyzed them in the past.

Looking forward, these circumstances suggest a prediction that the drive to break down racial barriers will not stall once a few victories are won, but will continue and intensify in the foreseeable future. However, there are some uncertain features of this development. First of all, it is unclear whether the conservatives, who were once the dominant leaders within the Negro community, are being completely supplanted by the protest leaders, or whether in the future there will continue to be a mixture of conservative and protest elements in Atlanta's Negro leadership. It is uncertain, because of increasing demands for equality from the masses, whether the aging conservative group will be replaced with leaders of similar stature and influence within the Negro community. If this does not occur, the present tactical balance within the Negro community will be altered in favor of the militants.

The full impact of such a change in Negro leadership on race relations in the city would depend in large measure on the reactions of the whites. Several local observers, when asked to comment on this prospect, emphasized that a new, younger and more liberal group of white leaders is emerging in the city to replace the older, more conservative whites. There is also a widely held impression in Atlanta that the majority of the white population has accepted, or at least is resigned to the end of segregation. These observers saw a prospect of diminishing resistance from the whites, faster integration, and improving race relations as the younger leaders of both races take control.

The accuracy of this prediction depends, to a large extent, upon the nature of the issues that face the community in the future, and upon the pliability of the whites as the Negroes begin aggressively attacking segregation in such potentially explosive areas as housing and employment. It also seems likely that in the future the Negro community may become more united behind the protest leaders, but this may not automatically result in an increased effectiveness in gaining their ends. This study brings into question the assumption commonly made that a weak minority within the society must maintain unity and solidarity if it is to be effective in gaining its objectives.

It seems clear that the Atlanta Negro community became more effective in breaking down the barriers of segregation after the militant, protest leaders came on the scene, even though their arrival caused considerable bickering and disunity among Negro leaders in the city. However, the protest leaders' outspoken desire to destroy the institutions of segregation, their habit of treating all issues in moral terms, and their willingness to employ force in the form of economic boycotts to gain their objective alienated them from the dominant white leadership. The conservative leaders were much more acceptable to the whites because they tended to concentrate primarily on improving the economic welfare of the Negro without demanding an immediate end to segregation. The conservative Negro leaders' primary interest in maintaining the institutions within the Negro community along with their antipathy for the protest leaders and their obvious disapproval of boycotts and demonstrations made them seem "responsible" in the eyes of the whites, and thus acceptable as bargaining agents. Therefore, it would seem that a Negro community in a Southern city is likely to be more effective in eliminating the institutions of segregation if it has both conservative and protest elements within its leadership. Without the protest leaders it will lack the capacity to precipitate tension through the use of boycotts, demonstrations, and other "direct action" techniques. And without the conservative leaders it is in danger of losing contact with the dominant white leaders and being unable to negotiate a peaceful, compromise solution to a racial crisis. Seen in this light, there seems to be a part to play in the Negro's fight for equality for both the more accommodating, conservative leaders and the liberal, protest leaders. As long as a broad agreement exists on the ultimate goals of equality and an end to racial discrimination, some disunity over the proper methods of social action may be positively desirable.

Jack L. Walker is presently (1989) Chair of the Department of Political Science at the University of Michigan. He has published widely and many of his articles have been frequently reprinted. His book with Joel D. Aberbach, *Race in the City: Political Trust and Public Policy in the New Urban System* was published by Little, Brown.

Notes

1. The research on which this essay is based was financed by a grant from the Iowa Citizenship Clearing House and the National Center for Education in Politics. Neither of them, of course, is responsible for any errors of fact or interpretation in this study.
2. Lewis M. Killian and Charles U. Smith, "Negro Protest Leaders in a Southern City," *Social Forces* (March, 1960), p. 257.
3. Leslie Dunbar, "Reflections on the Latest Reform of the South," *Phylon*, 22:253, Fall, 1961.
4. This case study is based on the record of the controversy found in the files of *The Atlanta Constitution*, *The Atlanta Journal*, *The Atlanta Daily World*, and *The Atlanta Inquirer*, and on a series of interviews with the principal actors conducted during April and May of 1962.
5. These demonstrations received nationwide attention, especially because of the arrest of Martin Luther King, Jr. and the series of events that led to the famous phone call to the King family from John F. Kennedy.
6. The principal actors in the sit-in controversy were interviewed at length, and frequently they voluntarily described themselves with such terms as "conservative" or "liberal." These self-identifications were used, along with an analysis of each participant's actions and statements during the dispute to decide which were conservatives and which were protest leaders.
7. It should not be surprising that the older leaders would be in sympathy with the goals of the students because the students' protests did not grow out of alienation from any of the society's basic orienting values except those, such as white supremacy, that underpin segregation. Searles and Williams found that the student protests "were precipitated by Negro students' reference to the white middle class as a standard of comparison . . ." they also discovered that: "Far from being alienated, the students appear to be committed to the society and its middle class leaders." Ruth Searles and J. Allen Williams, "Negro College Students' Participation in Sit-ins," *Social Forces*, 40: 219, March, 1962.
8. James Q. Wilson, "The Strategy of Protest," *Journal of Conflict Resolution* (September, 1961), p. 293.
9. Killian and Smith, p. 257.
10. Merrill Proudfoot, *Diary of a Sit-In* (Chapel Hill: University of North Carolina Press, 1962), pp. 111-112.
11. Clarence U. Patrick, *Lunch Counter Desegregation in Winston-Salem, North Carolina* (Pamphlet Distributed by the Southern Regional Council, 1960), p. 7.

Protest and Negotiation:

A Case Study of

Negro Leadership in Atlanta

JACK L. WALKER

Since the wave of sit-ins, freedom rides and other demonstrations by Negro college students in 1960 and 1961 there has been considerable speculation, both by journalists and social scientists, that a new, more "militant" type of leadership is emerging among American Negroes. Much attention has been focused on the activities of the students, and on such dramatic "protest leaders" as Martin Luther King, Jr., who, it is asserted, are steadily gaining the allegiance of the Negro masses at the expense of the older, more established community spokesmen.[1]

In this essay certain political attitudes and goals of a group of Negro civic leaders in Atlanta, Georgia will be described. An inquiry will be made into the motives of the student sit-in demonstrators, and the differences will be explored among Negro leaders of all kinds regarding goals and tactics. Also the socio-economic factors associated with their differing attitudes will be analyzed, and some speculation will be offered, based on the results of this study, about the future development of the leadership of the Negro community in Atlanta.

The description and analysis is based on material gathered during a series of interviews conducted with thirty-six Negro leaders in Atlanta during April and May, 1962.[2] The group selected for interviewing included the Negro leaders who were involved in the controversy over lunch counter segregation which lasted in Atlanta from March, 1960 when the first sit-ins took place, until September, 1961 when the lunch counters, rest rooms and other facilities in the major downtown department and variety stores were opened on a desegregated basis. The list includes all those who either led or helped to organize the sit-in demonstrations, picket lines and economic boycott that took place during the controversy, and all those who figured in attempts, either successful or unsuccessful, to negotiate an agreement to settle the dispute.[3]

The group selected for the study was drawn from almost every segment of Atlanta's Negro middle class, and it included ten businessmen, four college educators, four ministers, five lawyers, four social workers, two physicians, five staff members of civil rights groups, three student leaders, and one housewife. The group does not include, however, any labor leader or government employee, and it does not include a single teacher or administrator in the Atlanta public school system. The first two omissions are understandable since in Atlanta, outside of small segregated locals of the musicians and automobile workers, Negroes do not hold administrative posts in labor unions, and positions above the menial level in either the city, state, or national governments are held by only a tiny handful of Atlanta's Negroes. But the absence of the public school personnel is puzzling. There seems to be some fear among teachers that they might endanger their jobs by becoming involved in controversial public disputes. These apprehensions may or may not be justified. Further investigation suggested, however, that there was nothing about the sit-in controversy in particular that discouraged participation by the teachers. This group, which included the largest number of college trained professionals in the Negro community, seems to take little part in political affairs or protest movements of any kind.

This is a study of motives and political tactics; no effort was made to devise a method of identifying the "real" leaders of the community. The group that was interviewed does not include, by any means, all those in the Negro community who might have some legitimate claim to influence or leadership in civic or political affairs. Those who were chosen were the principal actors in the sit-in controversy, which was the most controversial single incident in the history of Atlanta's Negro community since World War Two. It is assumed that by concentrating on this set of dynamic circumstances a significant group of Negro community leaders has been obtained.

II

The spontaneous series of protest demonstrations by Negro college students that swept across the South in 1960 was a most significant manifestation of a growing impatience among Negroes all over the country with the progress being made to afford them social, economic, and political equality. Young Negroes were demonstrating that they were no longer willing to adjust their aspirations and their behavior to a system in which they were relegated to a second class status. Very little progress had been made through the regular channels of democratic decision-making toward removing racial bars to opportunity, even after the 1954 Supreme Court decision in the Brown case. Negroes were faced with the fact that they were still being denied the right to vote in some parts of the South, that there was continued, even increased, resistance from the segregationist whites, and that in the rest of the white community, all over the country, there seemed to be a general indifference to their plight. When these circumstances were viewed along with what seemed to them to be acquiescence to the status quo on the part of the established Negro leaders, the students became increasingly exasperated and impatient, and they went into the streets to obtain a hearing for their demands. The democratic process, the institutions based on discussion, negotiation and compromise, had proved unable to provide them with relief from the deprivations they suffered.

On February 1, 1960 several Negro students sat down at a lunch counter in Greensboro, North Carolina and refused to leave when told that the store did not serve Negroes. The manager is reported to have said: "They can just sit there. It's nothing to me." But within a week similar groups were sitting down in protest all across the South, and on February 17, 1960, the Georgia legislature responded to the growing movement by passing a special anti-trespass law.

On the campus of Atlanta University students were planning similar demonstrations as early as February 4, but they were persuaded by faculty members and an apprehensive administration to postpone their action until they had drawn up a statement of their grievances. This statement was quickly completed and printed in the form of a full page advertisement in all local newspapers on March 9, 1960 under the title: "An Appeal for Human Rights." The advertisement caused a sensation and it was commented on by politicians and public figures all over the country. This was followed on

March 15 by the first wide-spread sit-in demonstrations in Atlanta in which seventy-seven students were arrested under the new Georgia trespass law.

While their cases were pending in court the students began to work on several other projects. They mounted picket lines against food stores which had large Negro clienteles yet did not hire Negroes above the menial level; they held a series of meetings in Negro churches explaining the student movement and asking for support; they began publishing a weekly news sheet that eventually became a full fledged weekly newspaper, and on May 17, 1960 they gathered 1,400 students together to march on the state capitol in downtown Atlanta to celebrate the Supreme Court's 1954 anti-segregation decision. This march was diverted by Atlanta's Chief of Police to prevent the students from meeting a large, ugly crowd that had gathered at the capitol. When the students left for summer vacation tension was running high in the city.

During the summer the leaders of the student movement remained in Atlanta and continued organizational and propaganda work, and in the autumn, on October 19, 1960, they mounted widespread sit-ins once again, and once again large numbers of the demonstrators were arrested. The students refused to leave the jail on bail, and at this point the Mayor asked for, and was granted, a thirty-day truce period in which he promised to try to reach a settlement of the dispute.

The Mayor was unable even to get all the downtown merchants to meet to discuss the issue, and several other informal efforts to negotiate the dispute also failed. In part this was because of disagreements between the Negro leaders and in part because of the refusal of some white merchants to negotiate at all. The students resumed their sit-ins on November 25, 1960 and also organized a full-scale boycott of the downtown shopping area. A stalemate continued through the months of December and January, during which time most of the lunch counters remained closed and the boycott of the downtown stores remained in effect.

On February 1, 1961 the students, along with many adults, staged a march on the downtown area commemorating the anniversary of the beginning of the sit-in movement. Throughout this three month period the students, equipped with short-wave radios, had been sitting-in at lunch counters all over the city without incident. Either they had been ignored, or the counters had been closed, but on February 7, 1961 one restaurant manager in a federal office building invoked the trespass law and had the demonstrators arrested, and during the next three days arrests continued daily with the students refusing once again to come out on bail. A protest march and rally was planned to take place in front of the jail on February 19, and there was widespread fear that such a demonstration might result in a riot.

At this tense moment the student leaders themselves turned to one of the oldest, most respected Negro leaders who, by utilizing friendships he had with influential white leaders, was able to get negotiations started which eventually led to a settlement of the controversy. The agreement was announced on March 7, 1961 and after a bitter dispute within the Negro community it was accepted. It called for desegregation of the lunch counters after the school desegregation had been completed during the following fall. The counters were actually desegregated on September 27, 1961.

To some degree, the students staged their protest demonstrations because they no longer felt that they were legitimate participants in the democratic process. During the interviews students frequently expressed mistrust and suspicion of all politicians, both white and Negro, and their attitude seemed to be that, for the most part, the legislative bodies at both the state and national levels were simply institutions which had signs over their doors reading "whites only." The sit-in protests opened a new pathway though which these young Negroes could express their demands for equality. That they seized on this method with such enthusiasm and courage in the face of possible violence was a sign of their feeling of impotence within the established political system, and an indication of the depth of their frustrations.

III

One aspect of the student protests that was often commented on in the press was the extent to which the student leaders talked, and frequently acted, as if the adult Negro leaders were as much their enemies as the segregationist whites. This attitude among the students suggests the extent of their impatience with the progress made by the established Negro leaders, but it is also in part an indication of their distaste for the very system in which their leaders are participating. Gunnar Myrdal detected a similar attitude among "common Negroes," many of whom felt that their leaders were, "prepared to barter away their own honor and the interests of the group for a job or a handout." He explained this attitude as a displacement of hatred for the whole segregated society on to those who are participating in it and seem to be profiting from it in certain ways: "The Negro hates the Negro role in American society, and the Negro leader, who acts out this role in public life, becomes a symbol of what the Negro hates."[4]

In Atlanta the initial sit-in demonstrations took place virtually without the prior knowledge of the adult leaders, and several efforts to begin negotiations failed because of mutual suspicions and recriminations among the Negro leaders. In fact, when the final compromise settlement was announced in Atlanta, the first reaction of large numbers of students and adults was anger and rage expressed in claims that they had been "sold out." There were many baseless accusations that leaders (and at this point the students' leaders were included) had been bribed or had otherwise betrayed them. During the interviews much antipathy toward the adults who engaged in this final settlement of the sit-in controversy was encountered, and students frequently described them as "handkerchief heads," "accommodators," or "Uncle Toms."

In Atlanta, however, the adult Negro leaders do not form a monolithic bloc. Within the community there are divergences of opinion and political styles, and there is much disagreement, sometimes rather bitter in tone, over the proper tactics that should be used in gaining equality. Among the Negro leadership, such terms as "liberals" and " conservatives," "militants" and accommodators," "young turks" and "old guards" are used to describe the groupings within the Negro civic elite. The Negro leaders display considerable awareness that differences of opinion exist and committees or civic groups within the Negro community tend to be dominated by one or the other grouping. One older, very successful Negro businessman who has been very active in the city's politics describes himself as, "a mature conservative; one of the older heads," while a young physician who has become involved in political and civic work only in the last five years announces that, "I am one of your impatient Negroes."

Although those leaders usually labeled conservative by the community, and frequently by themselves as well, now dominate most of the organizations which deal exclusively with elections and political issues, such as the Atlanta Negro Voters League and the Westside Voters League, several other groups have grown up in recent years which are not under their control, such as the local chapter of the Southern Christian Leadership Council, a group of younger business and professional men called the Atlanta Committee for Cooperative Action, and a student organization called the Committee on an

Appeal for Human Rights. Also, in the last two years the local branch of the NAACP has shifted into relatively more militant hands.

The conservative group is quite aware that its power is being challenged and just as the students and the more militant adults manifest suspicion of the integrity of the conservative leaders, these men frequently question the motives and the honesty of the more militant group. The conservatives generally reject any suggestion that there are ideological differences within the Negro community, but they acknowledged that their authority is being questioned. Those challenging them are described variously as "immature," "unrealistic," "irresponsible," or by one man as: "a bunch of fanatics seeking power for power's sake."

This element of mutual distrust and the widely held impression that there is a contest for power going on showed up quite clearly in the opinions of the Negro leaders interviewed. In answers to the question: "What do you think are the greatest potential dangers to racial progress in the foreseeable future?" only three of the thirty subjects who responded mentioned some development in the white community as a danger. All the rest made reference to some condition in the Negro community. This tendency of Negroes to direct their attention to troubles among themselves rather than to the actions of the segregation forces in assessing the dangers to their continued progress emphasizes the importance of their internal dispute.

The argument seems to revolve around an evaluation of the degree of resistance in the white community to progress toward racial equality, and the stance that ought to be taken by the Negro in fighting this battle. A young physician argued that the drive for the end of racial discrimination was reaching a crucial point:

> This thing has begun now and it's like a snowball rolling and picking up speed. This progress will automatically follow *if* we just push hard enough! In the long view, if we just reach out, I think it's impossible to stop. Even the segregation people see this inevitable motion; you can see them beginning to rationalize a lot more than before and to accept defeat much more readily than before.

Seventeen of those responding to the question concerning the dangers they faced held variations on this view. They felt that the greatest danger to racial advancement was the possibility that the Negro community would relax in its drive for equality and be satisfied with only token gains. A lawyer in this group said:

The most important thing by far is stagnation. That is the danger that the Negro will lose his spirit and become satisfied with our present rate of progress; you know, stagnant tokenism.

Ten of the subjects also made reference to a problem within the Negro community, but they identified a different danger. In answer to this question an insurance executive said tersely:

That's simple. The greatest danger is the lack of character in Negro leadership. By that I mean the danger of selfishness and a disregard for the interests of the masses.

Those who shared this opinion were afraid that the wrong kind of leadership would gain control, a leadership not "realistic" enough, and one not dedicated to the interest of the people as they conceive of those interests. A professional social worker, widely known and very influential in politics, identified himself as a "realist above all else. That makes you a conservative in this community." He gave an emphatic answer to this question:

Without a doubt, the greatest danger is that the wrong people would gain control in the Negro community. We must not have people in control who want power for power's sake, or for personal, commercial or material gain. Now it is no sin to be ambitious and it's very hard to determine just when such conduct becomes improper, but you must not try to get anything for yourself out of political power. I have *never* done that! . . . In fact, I have a very religious commitment that a man will destroy himself if he uses his power selfishly . . . the only real power is in deeply consecrated people striving to promote the common good. Above all, we must not allow selfish leaders to destroy Negro solidarity in this city. The masses of the people in the Negro community are very poor and uneducated, and they are accustomed to strong, unified leadership.

The respondents who argued that there was a danger from the rise of selfish leaders were apparently expressing a fear of continued and greater Negro militancy and aggressiveness. When they were asked to name a Negro leader who posed such a threat they would usually refer to the most liberal and aggressive leaders in the Negro community. The average age of those who feared that irresponsible leaders might gain control was fifty-four, and they were generally labeled conservative by the community and by themselves. Most of those who expressed a fear that the Negroes in Atlanta might lose their militant spirit were generally thought to be liberal. Their average age was forty-one.

There were some exceptions here; one of those who expressed the most militant attitude and was very active in organizing economic boycotts against firms with discriminatory hiring policies shared the fear of selfish and corrupt leaders, and at the same time one of the best established Negro businessmen in the city, who was generally considered conservative, especially by the students, expressed apprehension that, "we will let up, become complacent with what we've got." Although the lines are blurred in these cases, there is generally found in the response to this question the outline of conflict; conflict between older men who are established in political and social position and consider themselves mature and realistic, and younger men who call themselves liberals and say that they are impatient for change and tired of compromise and evasion from the whites.

During the interviews no one was asked whether he considered himself to be liberal or conservative, but if in the course of the interview the subject referred to another person or group as conservative, liberal, radical, etc., he was immediately asked to define the term as he was using it. In the course of this line of questioning, he was asked to characterize other community leaders who were to be interviewed and sometimes, though less frequently than was expected, the subject would characterize himself. Of the thirty-six respondents, seven labeled themselves as liberals and eight labeled themselves as conservatives.

The ages of the self-identified liberals ranged from twenty-one to forty-three and their average age was thirty-one. The self-identified conservatives' average age was fifty-nine; the youngest was fifty and the oldest was sixty-five. Although these two groupings are sharply divided by age and although it seems generally true that as age increased militancy decreases among Negro leaders in Atlanta, it should be noted that this is not an invariable rule by any means. This study will show that the differences among those who did not voluntarily identify themselves are not nearly so sharp as between those who did. Also during the interviewing a student leader was encountered who displayed attitudes quite similar to the conservative group, and a minister and college teacher, both in their late fifties, displayed very militant attitudes.

IV

In an effort to establish the nature of the issues over which the Negro leaders are divided, each subject was asked to fill out two cards which were designed to reveal his position on the proper goals of the Negro's political and civic efforts in the city, and the most effective means available to achieve these goals. The cards were used on the assumption, shared by the most thoughtful participants in Atlanta's public life, both white and colored, that the Negro leaders are not in dispute over the goals toward which Negroes should strive, but only over the most effective tactics that should be used to achieve these goals.

The first card[5] with which the respondents were presented contained the following list of preferences:

( )   The chance to purchase homes anywhere in the city without restrictions.
( )   The freedom to use all public parks and to swim in the same places with whites.
( )   The chance at equal job opportunities, pay and promotion based on an individual's work and not on his race.
( )   The freedom to use all hotels and to eat in the same restaurants with whites.
( )   The end of segregation in the public schools.
( )   Equal treatment by the police and the courts.

In reference to this card each subject was asked: "If those changes affecting the way of life of the Negro in this city could come about immediately, which one would you like to see first, next, etc.?" The subject was asked to rank these preferences one through six.

There was reluctance to mark this card on the part of six of the subjects. One of the self-identified liberals objected to the implication that the Negro would agree any longer to obtain his rights piecemeal. Another man, who had been involved in many negotiations in the past, said he had developed the habit of asking for everything all at once, and the others argued that some of the alternatives were of equal importance and thus could not be put in rank order. These respondents were encouraged to mark the card anyway and all except one did so. The subject who refused simply wrote on it: "They are interlaced and interwoven."[6]

The results revealed that there was considerable agreement on the relative desirability of the various preferences presented:[7]

Liberals (N-7)	Conservatives (N-8)	Not Identified (N-19)	
3	4	3	(Housing)
5	6	5	(Public Parks)
1	1	1	(Job Opportunity)
6	5	6	(Hotels and Restaurants)
2	2	2	(Public Schools)
4	3	4	(Police and Courts

The most striking thing about the results of this test is the extent to which these groups are in agreement concerning the priority of increased economic opportunity and school desegregation as the two most important goals toward which the Negroes in Atlanta should strive. This result is somewhat in contrast to the findings of James Q. Wilson in Chicago. Wilson found that the protest or militant leaders tended to choose what he calls "status" ends rather than "welfare" ends when faced with a choice. A status end is one which seeks "the integration of the Negro into all phases of the community on the principle of equality—all Negroes will be granted the opportunity to obtain the services, positions, or material benefits of the community on the basis of principles other than race."[8] On the other hand a welfare end is described as "those which look to the tangible improvement of the community or some individuals in it through the provision of better services, living conditions, or positions."[9] The distinction is a subtle one, but Wilson explains it further by saying:

> Welfare and status ends are distinguished by, and defended in terms of, tangible versus intangible benefits, short-term versus long-term gains, and specific versus total solutions to the problems of the community. The differences [are] between those who advocate welfare ends, or *things*, and those who urge status ends or *principles* . . ."[10]

In Atlanta, although the liberals may deal with the problems of the community in moral, absolute terms more frequently than the conservatives, there seems to be a general agreement that welfare type goals are more important than status type goals. Even the liberals agreed that increased employment in city government should be accepted, even if it is placed on a quota basis. Also there was only one respondent who argued that Negroes should refuse to accept increased spending and development of new schools within the Negro community until all the schools were opened on the basis of equality.

There were, however, traces of the preference of status over welfare goals among the liberals. The liberals chose the right to purchase homes anywhere in the city above equal protection by the police which is the third choice of the conservatives. This could be explained by the different historical experience of the two groups. The older men usually talked at length about examples of police brutality and injustice that they had witnessed or experienced in the 1920's or 1930's, and they claim large responsibility for producing the present much more equitable situation through the use of their influence and their management of the political power of the Negro. One of the first breakthroughs they achieved after gaining the right to vote in the Democratic primary in 1946 was the obtaining of Negro policemen in the city in 1948. The younger men agree that the police in the city are remarkably fair and efficient, but they seem to take the situation somewhat for granted.

The younger men are more interested in desegregation of housing and, although they felt hopeless about the prospects, some spoke of getting a city ordinance establishing open occupancy. This attitude could be explained in part by a peculiar development in housing in the city, brought about for the most part by the older men. Atlanta is distinguished from most American cities by having extensive Negro suburbs. Large amounts of property on the West side of the town have been taken up by Negroes so that they are not encircled and bound to the central city by white suburban towns, and there are no man-made obstacles to their outward movement in that direction. But the well-kept sub-divisions that have sprung up on the West side since World War Two are a mark of segregation. They are as comfortable as those in the white neighborhoods, but they are part of a ghetto. The older men, in inaugurating the development of the West Side gave up efforts to penetrate the dominant white society, but the younger men, although indicating no intention of moving from the West Side, were obviously more eager to erase the stigma of the ghetto and the insult of segregated housing.

But the general preference among those respondents for welfare goals was underlined by the fact that the choices involving desegregation of parks, hotels and restaurants were placed at the bottom of the list by all groups. Moreover, none of the respondents took these things very seriously. This was true even of the student leaders whose names appeared as petitioners on a suit against the city calling for park desegregation that was pending in court at the time the interviews took place. The younger men picked the parks above hotels and restaurants, but in discussing the issue they seemed to be as much interested in gaining more parks for Negro neighborhoods as in desegregating all the city's recreational facilities.

When the respondents who marked the cards are arranged according to age the differences just discussed are reduced, and a broad unity of opinion is revealed:

45 years and Under (N-15)	46 years and Over (N-18)	
3	3	(Housing)
5	6	(Public Parks)
1	1	(Job Opportunity)
6	5	(Hotels and Restaurants)
2	2	(Public Schools)
4	4	(Police and Courts)

The test indicates that thoughtful local observers are correct when they suggest that there is little dispute among Negroes in Atlanta concerning the goals toward which they should be working. It would seem that among the leaders examined here this is true to a remarkable extent. Although the liberals may find the status differentials between whites and Negroes in Atlanta more galling and frustrating than the older conservatives, all the leaders, both young students and older bankers and business leaders, agree that the economic goals—increased employment opportunity and nondiscriminatory advancement policies—should have the highest priority for action.

V

Once each subject had marked the first card he was presented with a second one on which were listed the following preferences:

( )   Private negotiations with influential whites.
( )   Economic Boycotts.
( )   Efforts to encourage increased voting among Negroes.
( )   Demonstrations of protest such as sit-ins and marches.
( )   Civil Rights suits in Courts of Law.

In reference to this card each subject was told: "Listed on that card are various kinds of action that can be used to gain the changes in the Negroes' way of life that were listed on the first card. Which of the methods of bringing about change listed on this card do you think is most effective, next, etc?" Once again the subject was asked to mark the card one through five.

This test was designed on the assumption that debate among Negro leaders in Atlanta had reached such a stage that those most committed to a political style would mark the card immediately, without extensive consideration. This assumption proved largely correct, again testifying to the emotional intensity of the dispute going on within the Negro community. Those who had voluntarily identified themselves as conservatives or liberals tended to mark this card without hesitation, while those who had been reluctant to mark the first card usually objected even more strenuously to this one.

Eight subjects hesitated or objected to marking this card. One of these was a self-identified liberal who argued that voting should not be included along with the other alternatives because increased voting among Negroes had primarily a long range influence and made very little impact on day to day struggles involving particular issues, especially where private businesses or institutions were involved. The rest argued, in one way or another, that no one tactic was necessarily more effective than any other. The relative effectiveness, they asserted, depended entirely on the particular situation and the issues at stake; therefore, any one of the tactics listed on the card might be the most effective, or the least effective, depending on the circumstances involved. The same gentleman who refused to mark the first card seemed to have this approach to social action, and he refused to mark the second card as well. This time he wrote on it: "All are important and effective."

But the card was marked by most of the subjects without any objections. In fact, several accompanied their marking with such comments as: "This is simple enough," or "Well, I see my first choice right off." The self-identified groups ranked the alternatives in the following way.[11]

Liberals (N-7)	*Conservatives* (N-8)	
5	2	(Negotiation)
1	5	(Boycotts)
2	1	(Voting)
3	4	(Demonstrations)
4	3	(Law Suits)

The contrasts here are striking and the results of this test offer strong evidence that the dispute between the older, better established group and the younger group is more than simply a struggle for power and prestige. At least among these deeply committed individuals a sharp dispute is in process over the proper tactics that should be used to carry on their fight for equality.

There is not too much disagreement between the two groups over the importance of increasing the number of Negro voters although the more militant group places it second in importance. However, attitudes toward this subject are more divergent than the results of the test reveal. The conservatives usually accompanied their selection of this alternative as their first choice with a lecture on the power of the ballot which was punctuated with stories illustrating how much their situation had changed since the end of the white primary in 1946. One story concerning the mayor's rather contemptuous treatment of their plea for more street lights in the early 1940's which he dismissed with the remark: "Come back to see me when you have 10,000 votes," was frequently repeated.

The liberal group, however, seemed very reluctant to place voting high on the list although they acknowledged its importance. One of them said:

> Voting is damned important of course . . . but it's over-rated by Negroes, I think. Even with the votes you can't just sit back as some people in this town think. You don't get things without pushing and shoving.

There was a difference of opinion about the efficacy of law suits. Both groups thought that law suits were important and effective means of gaining civil rights victories, but once again the liberals argue that they are not very useful against privately imposed segregation. One young lawyer, although he was not in the self-identified liberal group, listed law suits fourth most effective and stated the objections of the militants quite well by saying:

> The Federal courts seem to be slowly expanding their definition of what constitutes a public activity or function, but they aren't in any hurry to do it. That's a hot one you know—very controversial. Anyway, we are out to get segregation now, not just legal segregation.

The kernel of the dispute between the two groups, however, is their contrasting attitudes toward the possibility of working out compromises with the white community, and in general their attitude toward the present system of settling racial disputes. The conservatives believe strongly in the importance of private negotiations with white leaders, while the liberals place this tactic last on their list. The liberals consider economic boycotts the most effective means of getting their way while the conservatives placed it at the bottom of their list. One member of the conservative group stated flatly: "Man, I just don't like this boycotting—I don't care who's doing it—I just don't think it's right!" The two groups have opposite opinions on the so-called "direct action" techniques. Some of the conservatives seem to reject them almost without qualification, but if such means must be used they prefer protest demonstrations over boycotts. However, the liberals are not even as enthusiastic about protest demonstrations as the results of the test might suggest. They believe that their usefulness in Atlanta is decreasing primarily because the white population is becoming accustomed to seeing Negroes picketing and demonstrating and has begun to ignore them. The leaders of the sit-in demonstrations in Atlanta were quite sensitive to coverage of their activities by the press and they were aware that news of demonstrations was taken off the front page and relegated to the more inconspicuous parts of the newspaper as the controversy dragged on.

When the results of this test from all the respondents are examined the differences between the younger and older leaders is moderated somewhat:

45 and Under (N-15)	*46 and Over* (N-18)	
3	3	(Negotiations)
2	4	(Boycotts)
1	1	(Voting)
5	5	(Demonstrations)
4	2	(Law Suits)

Differences between the two age groups still exist, but the principal one, the younger groups' preference for economic boycotts over private negotiations with the whites and civil rights suits is less sharply defined than previously. Efforts to increase Negro voting is considered the most effective tactic by both groups, and the older leaders now have a lower rating for private negotiations with the whites and find boycotts more effective than demonstrations, though by a small margin.

VI

Emerging from these interviews is a spectrum of opinion of the effectiveness of various techniques of social action within a significant segment of the leadership of the Atlanta Negro community. There seems to be considerable agreement among these leaders on the goals toward which Atlanta's Negroes ought to strive, but at opposite extremes of the spectrum widely respected leaders exist who disagree very sharply with each other over the tactics to be used in pursuing these goals. These conflicting opinions are a reflection of differences in historical experience between the two groups and also they are a function of their differing positions and occupations within the Negro community.

Of those who identified themselves as conservatives in this study there was one college administrator, one social worker, and six businessmen. These men expressed an aversion for direct action techniques and boycotts and a strong preference for private negotiations with influential whites. They have built up good contacts with the whites over the years, and pride themselves on their ability to speak directly to the top white leaders in the city.

The conservatives feel that their position bars them from taking an active part in protest demonstrations because these public displays of discontent naturally cause bitterness and rancor and tend to destroy the cordial, settled

47

atmosphere which they feel is a necessary precondition to effective negotiations. They also have worked hard to build institutions such as the Y.M.C.A., the Urban League and many churches which depend heavily on contributions from influential whites, and during the boycott that accompanied the sit-in affair in Atlanta some of these organizations began to lose white contributors as tension mounted. To some extent the conservatives have each made adjustments to the traditional position of the Negro in southern society. In varying measures they have given up efforts to penetrate the dominant white society and consequently they have a greater commitment to the institutions of the Negro community.

The businessmen among the conservatives have frequent dealings with influential whites in the city; both the bank and the savings and loan association operated by Negroes in Atlanta have very sizable deposits from white customers. In fact, to a large extent, the power of the conservatives depends on their influence with the white community. They are spokesmen for the Negro community primarily because they have gained white recognition and favor, although their own achievements placed them in a position to be chosen for this role. Because of this process of selection, the liberals regard the conservatives with almost the same hostility they have for the whites, if not more so. They complain that the conservatives' power is based essentially on the Negro's fear of the power of the white man. They think that the established leaders have profited from the injustices of segregation by trading their human dignity for the opportunity to represent the whites within the Negro community.

The younger men are not so directly engaged in activities and institutions that serve the whole community as are the conservatives. Among the group that voluntarily identified themselves as liberals there were two individuals who worked for civil rights or Negro improvement groups, one college teacher, one social worker, one physician, one student leader, and one businessman. These men deal more exclusively with the Negro community than the conservatives, yet at the same time they do not feel as much committed to its maintenance; in fact, they hate all that it stands for. Their work brings them into close contact with the social, economic and political deprivations suffered by the Negro, and they tend to concentrate on these injustices and have fewer reasons to try to protect institutions, both charitable and commercial, that presently exist in the Negro community. They are under less compulsion than the conservatives to act with restraint or to compromise their demands in order to make limited material gains or to promote the fortunes of Negro businessmen. In this sense they stand outside the economic and social life of the established community and they try to keep the dominant leaders, both white and colored, at arm's length, guarding against being too friendly with politicians and certainly never asking them for favors or help of any kind. They try to conduct their affairs strictly on the basis of their moral principles, and for these reasons conservatives frequently regard them as "irresponsible" and find their attitudes toward politics and community leaders "unrealistic" or "hateful." One member of the conservative group, who has a reputation as a good tactician and organizer, acknowledged the importance of the student protest in bringing "more integration in less than two years than we gained in ten," but he argued that "they will never get anything done on their own because they are cut off; they work in a righteous vacuum over there."

The whites also play a large part in selecting the liberal or militant leaders just as they do in choosing the conservative spokesmen. However, it is important to the liberal leaders to become the objects of hostility from the whites, not of their beneficence. At the beginning of the sit-in protests in Atlanta, when student leaders from several organizations on the Atlanta University campus seemed to competing for control of the new movement, they began vying with each other in making bold, uncompromising public statements, and when they met privately with a leading white merchant they tried to out do each other in challenging him and impressing him with their determination. It is important, to the student leaders in particular, to have the badge of at least one jail sentence for breaking a segregation law, and Martin Luther King, Jr. could have asked for nothing better than to have been bitterly attacked by the Governor of Georgia when he decided in 1960 to move from Montgomery, Alabama to Atlanta. The liberals thrive on the antagonism of the whites, while the conservatives court their good favor.

The rest of the Negro leaders, those not identified with either the conservatives or liberals, are caught in a maze of conflicting influences stemming from their occupations, their age and historical experiences, their functions within the Negro community and their relations with the whites. These men, spread across the spectrum of opinion between the self-identified liberals and conservatives, display several different combinations of attitudes and action.

Several leaders claimed agreement with the liberals' approach to political tactics yet did not identify themselves as members of the liberal group. During the sit-in controversy these men did not actually involve themselves in the public demonstrations or in advising the student leaders. They marked the attitude cards in a way that suggested their liberal views, but they did not endorse these views with action. Typical of this group was a college teacher in his late fifties who expressed strong approval of the sit-in demonstrations and the boycott. He has been involved in voter registration drives ever since the end of the white primary in 1946 and he is a member of many other community organizations, but he also has close relationships and friendships with many of the leading conservatives. He excused himself for not participating more actively in the sit-in controversy by saying: "They always seemed to schedule meetings when I had obligations at school." Another member of this group is a social worker in his middle forties who has very militant attitudes and is a member of several organizations which are dominated by the liberals, but who works for an agency which depends heavily on financial support from the white community and so he maintains a "realistic" alliance with the conservative leaders and did not participate directly in the protest actions.

On the other side of the spectrum are leaders who hold conservative views but who did not criticize the actions of the demonstrators during the sit-ins or make efforts to bring the protests to an end. A lawyer in his early forties fits into this category. He believed strongly that community disputes should be settled through negotiation and felt that the demonstrators frequently acted unrealistically or recklessly during the sit-in dispute. But he did not have a high regard for the established community leaders, and since he is a relatively young man who was not born in Atlanta, he does not have a close relationship with the most influential conservatives. He was called on by the students for legal advice at one point during the sit-in controversy, and he gave it, but otherwise he took no part in the dispute.

Standing in the center of the spectrum is a third group of leaders whose attitudes and actions during the sit-in controversy were ambiguous. One such leader is a young but very successful businessman who has many friends among the liberals, but also has the confidence of several conservatives. He holds high offices in organizations dominated by both sides and a white observer described him as: "the best case of a man over there who has a foot in all camps." This man marked the attitude card concerning tactics three different ways, describing a set of situations that would call for each ranking. Leaders of this sort tended to be least committed to a particular tactical weapon or technique, but not necessarily the less effective in obtaining their goals. When faced with a social or political conflict these men begin thinking of ways to limit the scope of their difficulties and extend the possible alternatives for action. They speak mostly of partial solutions to outstanding disputes and seem to think primarily in terms of the short-run, immediate consequences that might result from their decisions.

This group of leaders in the middle, subject to cross-pressures generated by the ambiguous circumstances in which they find themselves, serve as a balancing force between the more single-minded liberals and conservatives. These men who are not fully committed to either side, through their personal friendships and their memberships in various organizations, tend to moderate the sharp differences of opinion over tactics that exist within the Negro community. Because of their formal and informal efforts, organizational rivalry and bickering is reduced, and the Negro's attack on the institutions of segregation in Atlanta is more unified and effective.

VII

This study of Negro leadership is confined to the description of circumstances existing in Atlanta, Georgia. But unless case studies generate hypotheses which can be examined and tested in other settings they do not make a significant contribution to the study of political behavior. No effort is made in this study to arrive at generalizations concerning the leadership in all southern Negro communities. In fact, until more progress is made in developing the comparative study of metropolitan political systems all observations concerning the similarities and differences between various communities will necessarily be vague and purely impressionistic. But, even with these reservations, several conclusions are suggested which could be studied fruitfully in other Negro communities:

(1) Liberal and conservative Negro leaders in the South are in essential agreement on the ranking of goals toward which the Negro community should strive. Although differences of emphasis exist, there seems to be a general consensus that it is more important at this time to improve the welfare of the Negro community and increase the services available to it than to fight to completely eliminate racial discrimination in all phases of the life of the city. Presently welfare goals are more important than status goals.

(2) The disunity presently existing among Negro leaders in Atlanta is not primarily the result of a clash between two generations holding contrasting

political attitudes. Although in this study the average age of the self-identified liberals was lower than the average age of the self-identified conservatives, when the data from the attitude cards were tabulated according to age groupings, broad agreement between younger and older leaders was discovered. Age is not the most important factor distinguishing the antagonists among Negro leaders.

(3) Liberal and conservative leaders disagree primarily over the tactics to be employed in achieving their goals. At least when faced with a sharp, emotional community dispute involving the issue of racial discrimination, the Negro leaders divide between those who want to use aggressive, "direct action" techniques and those who wish to negotiate "behind the scenes" with influential whites. Caught between these extremes are leaders who act infrequently and reluctantly, or who seem to be called in only to ratify decisions made by others. Some of these men do not take a vigorous and direct role in such controversies because they are not firmly committed to either tactical approach while others find themselves enmeshed in a conflicting web of cross-pressures which restrains them from acting on strongly held opinions.

At the center of the spectrum are leaders who consciously avoid direct identification with any one approach and who endeavor to maintain contact with all parties to the dispute. They measure the circumstances and try to fit their actions to the exigencies of the moment, always trying to maintain their focus on short-run possibilities and solutions.

(4) The isolation of the leadership of the two racial groups, brought on by segregation, is a serious and potentially disruptive weakness in the social structure of a city with a large Negro population. There are no social contacts between white and Negro leaders in Atlanta, and residential segregation places their homes far apart. There are numerous Negro owned businesses, and the institutions within the Negro community are so well developed that it is possible for a Negro to live a distinctly middle class life in Atlanta while having only marginal contacts with the whites. In such a situation, if a crisis arises involving the crucial issues of race, communication between the two racial groups, which is normally rather tenuous and formal, becomes very hard to maintain, and it is even more difficult to establish the conditions in which negotiation of the difficulties that caused the crisis can take place.

During the controversy over the sit-in demonstrations in Atlanta such a breakdown in communications occurred. It was caused in large measure by the inability of the Negroes to agree among themselves, the militant attitude of the student leaders which antagonized many of the whites, and the stubborn refusal of certain white businessmen to discuss the matter at all. It was at this juncture that the student leaders turned to one of the oldest, most respected Negro leaders, who was widely considered to be a conservative although he did not voluntarily identify himself as such when interviewed. He contacted an influential white lawyer with whom he had a cordial relationship, and together these two men were able to initiate negotiations that eventually led to a settlement of the controversy.

(5) Thus when the Negro community becomes involved in a struggle against the institutions of segregation, both the liberal and the conservative leaders can perform useful roles:

(a) The liberal group's function is, literally, to start fights they are unable to finish. They are able to create a crisis, but are frequently unable to resolve it because they have no basis for contact with the dominant white leaders. As James Q. Wilson suggests, one of the inherent difficulties in the use of protest action is: "that the discretion of the protest leader to bargain after he has acquired the resources with which to bargain is severely limited by the means he was forced to employ in order to create those resources."[12] From the beginning of the sit-in dispute in Atlanta the leading merchants refused to negotiate directly with the demonstrators whom they considered to be irresponsible troublemakers.

(b) The conservatively inclined leaders, utilizing their reputations and the connections they have built up with the white community through the years, have the function of resolving the crisis situation created by the protest leaders. In the Atlanta dispute even the antagonism between the two groups was functional because it made the conservatives seem more reliable and responsible in the eyes of the whites and so they were still able to act as negotiators when both sides were ready to compromise.

(c) Those leaders in the middle, who do not identify completely with either the conservative or the protest leaders, have the function of moderating this conflict over tactics. Some individuals find themselves in this situation because they are subject to cross-pressures which restrain them from becoming attached to either side in the controversy. Others are not committed because they have a flexible attitude toward social action which prompts them to regard all tactical weapons as potentially useful. Regardless of the influences that put them in this position, however, these leaders in the middle provide both formal and informal links between the conservative and protest leaders.

(d) Before the leaders can perform their various functions, of course, the liberal group must create a serious crisis through its actions. Until a genuine threat to the public order and reputation of the community exists, the dominant whites are unlikely to be willing to negotiate concessions with the conservative leaders.

VIII

The situation in Atlanta does not seem to have been unique. Something of this same kind of unanticipated cooperation and sharing of functions between liberal and conservative Negro leaders seems to have taken place during the sit-in controversy in Knoxville, Tennessee. Negotiation began initially there without any demonstrations, but broke down after four tedious months of talks. Sit-ins began on June 9, 1960 and a boycott was started five days later on June 14. Merrill Proudfoot describes a meeting of the executive committee of the protest movement which took place on July 2, 1960 after about three weeks of demonstrations. The meeting was attended by the president of Knoxville College, who had not been involved in planning or staging the demonstrations, and he revealed that he had been contacted by an official of the Knoxville Chamber of Commerce who informed him that there was a movement underway to reopen negotiations. Proudfoot rather indignantly comments:

> The circuitous means of communicating with one another has lent a comic-opera aspect to the way this major community problem has been handled. It would seem sensible for one of the merchants to have called Crutcher or James, the leaders of the demonstrations and said, "come on down and let's talk!" Instead the merchants hint to the Chamber of Commerce official that they might be willing; he contacts not Crutcher or James, but Colston—the one person in the Negro community who has the greatest status . . . and he in turn makes the contact within the Negro community."[13]

Also when a negotiating team was created to formulate the final agreement to desegregate, Colston was included once again, but this time he was accompanied by Crutcher. Although the description is not so complete it seems that a similar process operated at Winston-Salem, North Carolina where the agreement to desegregate the lunch counters was not formulated by the protest leaders. Clarence H. Patrick reports that:

> The demonstrators several times sought unsuccessfully for someone to organize and mediate a meeting between them and the store managers in an attempt to resolve the antisegregation movement on the basis of some mutual agreement. The leaders of the protest never met, as a group, with the managers of the stores where the protests occurred.[14]

The evidence presented here suggests that in some Southern Negro communities a kind of tactical balance presently exists with both conservative and protest leaders playing a part in the fight for equality. However, there is no evidence that the period of change and transition in Negro leadership in Atlanta has ended. In fact, a major unsettling force seems to be developing beneath the level of leadership. Almost all the leaders interviewed, including the conservatives, felt that expectations are rising perceptibly throughout the Negro community as a result of recent successful attacks on the institutions of segregation. The Negro masses, who have traditionally been apathetic toward politics and efforts to fight segregation, seem to be gaining hope that change is possible and are shaking off the mood of cynical resignation that has paralyzed them in the past.

Looking forward, these circumstances suggest a prediction that the drive to break down racial barriers will not stall once a few victories are won, but will continue and intensify in the foreseeable future. The progress toward desegregation which has recently taken place in Atlanta, such as that in the public parks, buses, libraries, and lunch counters, has been in areas which this study has shown are least important to the Negro leaders, while large scale integration of the public schools, housing segregation and discrimination in employment, which they consider most important, have yet to be approached on a broad scale.

Whatever the prospects for the future, however, the indications are that the issue of racial discrimination will dominate Atlanta's politics for some time to come. In fact, as the younger Negroes begin to look outside the boundaries of the Negro ghetto and yearn for integration into the dominant community, they are not likely to become satisfied until their status or social ranking is arrived at rationally, and until they are judged on the basis of their personal attainments, not merely on the basis of their color. A young lawyer expressed this yearning for community recognition and status when he said: "I want to practice as a lawyer, not as a Negro lawyer." Even more poignantly this mood was expressed by a college teacher who spoke as he gazed out the window of his office at Atlanta University:

> You know, I've lived in this town for twenty years now, and I love it here. But the worst thing about it here is the isolation. Why, there are white people who drive by this school every day on their way to work who don't even know what it is. They think it's a hospital or a housing project, and, you know, the very worst thing is they don't take time to find out. They just don't care.

Notes

1. The literature is voluminous, but among the most interesting journalistic efforts are: Hodding Carter, "The Young Negro is a New Negro," *The New York Times Magazine*, May 1, 1960, p. 11; Helen Fuller, "Southern Students Take Over," *The New Republic*, 142: 14-16, May 2, 1960; Louis Lomax, "The Negro Revolt Against the Negro Leaders," *Harper's Magazine*, June, 1960, p. 41; Kenneth Rexroth, "Students Take Over," *The Nation*, 191: 4-9, July 2, 1960; Dan Wakefield, *Revolt in the South* (New York, Grove Press, 1960); Howard Zinn, "Finishing School for Pickets," *The Nation*, 191: 71-73, August 6, 1960. Scholarly contributions are not so numerous, but of special interest are: M. Elaine Burgess, *Negro Leadership in a Southern City* (Chapel Hill, University of North Carolina Press, 1962); Tilman Cothran and William Phillips, "Negro Leadership in a Crisis Situation," *Phylon*, Vol. 22 (Summer, 1961), pp. 107-118; Leslie Dunbar, "Reflections on the Latest Reform of the South," *Phylon*, Vol. 22 (Fall, 1961), pp. 249-257; Lewis M. Killian and Charles U. Smith, "Negro Protest Leaders in a Southern Community," *Social Forces* (March, 1960), pp. 253-260.
2. This research was made possible by the support of the Iowa Citizenship Clearing House and the National Center for Education in Politics. Neither of them, of course, is responsible for any errors of fact or interpretation in this study.
3. The list was compiled from the record of the controversy found in the files of *The Atlanta Constitution, The Atlanta Journal, The Atlanta Daily World*, and *The Atlanta Inquirer*. Each of those identified in the newspaper reports as leaders or important participants was asked to look over the list and add the names of anyone who had led the protest demonstrations, or participated in negotiating sessions of any kind during the controversy. Only two names were added to the list in this way that were not found in the newspaper reports.
4. Gunnar Myrdal, *An American Dilemma* (New York; Harper and Brothers, 1944) p. 744.
5. This first card is a slightly modified version or a card used by Lewis M. Killian and Charles M. Grigg, "Rank Orders of Discrimination of Negroes and Whites in a Southern City," *Social Forces* (March, 1961), pp. 235-239.
6. None of the respondents said he had no preference or that he did not care about one of the changes, but there were those who said that one of the alternatives was no longer a problem (usually this was equal treatment by the police and the courts) at least within the Atlanta city limits. These subjects were encouraged to assign a number anyway, but two refused. In those cases the number six was arbitrarily assigned to the category the subject had omitted.
7. To arrive at a group ranking for this test, the responses of each individual to each of the preferences presented on the card were simply added to the responses of all others in this group. A group ranking was assigned to each preference on the basis of this composite score.
8. James Q. Wilson, *Negro Politics* (Glencoe, The Free Press, 1960), p. 185.

9. *Ibid.*

10. *Ibid.*, p. 186.

11. Among those who did not identify themselves as liberal or conservative there was much disagreement on this card. Some individuals in this group placed lawsuits first in effectiveness, and others put voting at the top of their lists. These leaders are not included in this chart because to lump them together in a composite grouping would give a false picture of unanimity among them.

    The average rankings of the self-identified liberals and conservatives are close to the actual rankings made by most of the respondents. The range of choices on each alternative was narrow. Negotiations were ranked between 3 and 5 by the liberal respondents and either 1 or 2 by the conservatives. Boycotts were ranked either 1 or 2 by the liberals and either 4 or 5 by the conservatives. Increased voting was ranked either 1 or 2 by the conservatives and between 1 and 5 by the liberals. Demonstrations were ranked from 2 to 4 by the liberals and either 4 or 5 by the conservatives. Law suits were ranked from 2 to 5 by the liberals and from 1 to 3 by the conservatives.

12. James Q. Wilson, "The Strategy of Protest," *Journal of Conflict Resolution* (September, 1961), p. 293.

13. Merrill Proudfoot, *Diary of a Sit-in* (Chapel Hill, University of North Carolina Press, 1962), pp. 111-112.

14. Clarence H. Patrick, *Lunch Counter Desegregation in Winston-Salem, North Carolina* (Pamphlet Distributed by the Southern Regional Council, 1960), p. 7.

Sit-Ins in Atlanta:
A Study in
the Negro Revolt

JACK L. WALKER

Introduction:
The Roots of the Protest

In recent years a major social upheaval has been taking place in the southern United States. The institutions of racial segregation, the basis of social life in the region for over one-half century, have been crumbling amidst the clamor of impassioned political oratory and the chanting of exuberant Negro demonstrators. Young, energetic, and profoundly impatient Negro leaders have arisen in communities throughout the South. Often taking the white leaders by surprise, they have managed to shake the foundations of social organization in their towns and cities. Although the outcome of the revolt they have been leading is still unclear, by their efforts they have ensured that the South will never be the same again.

The causes of the Negro revolt in the South are extremely complicated. As with many other revolutions, it took place even though the general level of economic well-being among Negroes was rising and even though the barriers of segregation were already beginning to crumble. Although the revolt had many separate roots, two general influences must be identified as necessary, if not sufficient, conditions. First, the economy of the area has been undergoing great changes during the last three decades. The southern countryside has been transformed as agriculture has been mechanized, and large numbers of sharecroppers and field hands have deserted the land for jobs—or at least the hope of jobs—in industry. As the popular saying goes: "Cotton is going West, cattle are coming East, Negroes are going North, and Yankees are coming South." In a comparatively short period of time, the South has given up its reliance on cash crop agriculture and has begun to urbanize and industrialize with almost bewildering speed. These developments have been paralleled by the creation of an increasingly large middle class among southern Negroes. Businesses and educational institutions have developed within urban Negro communities; and from these sources, during the last twenty-five years, a reservoir of potential community leaders has been created. The development of an aggressive and talented middle class within an emerging minority group has traditionally been an important first step toward political and social integration into American society. Numbers alone have seldom been sufficient to guarantee success in achieving recognition from the dominant elements in a democratic political system. Until the appearance of skillful, ambitious leaders who are willing to expend considerable amounts of time, money, and energy organizing the group for political action, the potential power of a group remains untapped.

Atlanta, Georgia, has been, in many ways, a major focal point for both of these broad changes in southern society. Since the 1850s, when it became a railroad terminus, the city has been growing in importance, and its population has been steadily increasing. By the first decade of the twentieth century, it had recovered from the destruction of the Civil War and was a thriving, bustling industrial town. In the years since World War II, it has undergone its most rapid development and has become one of the country's major cities. Between 1950 and 1960 the population of the Atlanta metropolitan area grew from 726,989 to 1,017,188, an increase of 39.9 percent in a single decade.

The Atlanta Negro community has grown along with the city, and while the percentage of Negroes living in the total metropolitan area has been decreasing, the percentage of Negroes living in the central city has been increasing. In 1960 it climbed to 38.8 percent. Also, the median income of the city's Negro community has been slowly rising. For an increasing number of Negroes, opportunities have developed to attain incomes which provide them with solid middle class living standards from jobs in the city's rapidly expanding public school system, its Negro controlled colleges, some federal agencies, and in the Negro owned financial institutions and businesses.

The predominantly Negro Atlanta University Center has more than 3,600 students and 200 full-time faculty members. The Center includes four undergraduate Colleges—Clark, Morehouse, Morris Brown, and Spelman; the interdenominational Theological Center; and Atlanta University, with its Professional Schools of Business, Education, Library Service, and Social Work, and the Graduate School of Arts and Sciences. Because of the presence of such institutions in the community, Atlanta has more Negro professionals than any other southern city.

Negro leadership has also been influenced and stimulated by the presence in the city of an unusual number of social workers, professional civil rights organizations, and other groups devoted to improving race relations. Just as the city serves as a headquarters for many business corporations and government agencies, it also is the southeastern regional headquarters for the National Association for the Advancement of Colored People, the Urban League, the National Students Association, B'nai B'rith, and several religious groups working on social problems. Atlanta also serves as the headquarters for the influential Southern Regional Council, Martin Luther King's Southern Christian Leadership Conference, and the militant Student Nonviolent Coordinating Committee. The existence of these regional agencies prompts their Atlanta chapters to attempt to set high standards of performance, and the constant communication which takes place between the regional and local Negro leadership serves to raise the level of aspirations and political skills among Negroes in the city.

As the level of aspiration has risen among middle class Negroes in Atlanta, however, their frustration and resentment at the barriers of segregation have also increased. As more Negroes complete high school and college in the city, the problem of *underemployment* has risen. After the individual makes the personal sacrifices necessary to obtain an education, his inability to find an opportunity to use his skills is a source of great humiliation and frustration. Atlanta's newspapers list large numbers of job openings for whites, but only a handful for Negro men, and these are in menial capacities such as car washer or porter. Almost all major unions in the city either deny Negroes membership or have segregated locals. Only a handful of Negro physicians practice in the city, and they are denied membership in the local medical society—and thus excluded from membership in the American Medical Association. The city's seventeen Negro dentists are excluded from the American Dental Association in the same fashion. Most graduates of Atlanta University must leave the city to find employment commensurate with their skills. During a four year period in the late 1950s, Atlanta University's School of Social Work had 124 graduates, of whom only seven could find employment in Atlanta. Most Negro college graduates in Atlanta may look forward to jobs only in the public schools or the post office. But in the Atlanta post office, only about five percent of the supervising positions are held by Negroes. Of the postal carriers, eighty percent are now Negroes; and of that number, over sixty percent have college degrees.

Even those middle class Negroes who have important and challenging jobs, however, are not afforded the community recognition and status that whites in similar positions receive. Since World War II, advertisers have discovered the so-called "Negro market," and have made special efforts through radio, magazines, newspapers, and television to encourage Negroes to strive toward middle class living standards. But together with an increased yearning for material living standards also develops the passionate wish to enjoy the social status of the American middle class. And once the necessary education and income for middle class living is obtained, the social and political restrictions of segregation, which are imposed on all Negroes, regardless of class, become almost intolerable. As the economic and educational attainments of Atlanta's Negro middle class increased, their sense of *relative* deprivation increased at the same time because they began to judge their achievements by the standards of the white middle class rather than those of the Negro community alone. Especially among the students and young adults, those who had not adopted an accommodating stance and had refused to lose hope that broad changes were possible, a sense of resentment began to rise at being unavoidably locked into a subordinate status.

This sense of resentment erupted in 1960 in a spontaneous series of protest demonstrations by Negro college students which swept across the South. Young Negroes were demonstrating that they were no longer willing to adjust their aspirations and behavior to a social system in which they had only second class status. Older Negro leaders had carried on the struggle for equality through the regular channels of democratic decision making, but little tangible progress had been made, even after the 1954 Supreme Court decision against school segregation. Negroes were faced with the same denials of economic opportunity; they were still being prevented from voting in many parts of the South; and there was continued—even increased—resistance from the segregationist whites. In Congress, the southern legislators in their "Southern Manifesto" had called for defiance of the Supreme Court's decision; throughout the South, membership in the White Citizens Councils was growing; President Eisenhower had taken an ambiguous and equivocal stand on civil rights and desegregation; involved battles were taking place in the courts which seemed to lead always to delay and more delay; even the civil rights bill passed by the Congress in 1957 offered little hope for an immediate end to segregation. Outside the South, white political leaders called for an end to segregation, but counseled patience and restraint and stressed the importance of order and peaceful change. The older, established Negro leaders were genuinely dissatisfied and desirous of change, but they confined their efforts within the traditional, respectable, public arenas; they refused to make any radical departures. Established leaders in both the white and Negro communities, in the North and South, shared the prevailing political atmosphere of the 1950s, in which dissenting opinions were suspect, controversy was muted, and change seemed remote, if not impossible. The younger Negroes began to realize that in this atmosphere segregation might thrive for another generation or more.

The sit-in protests opened a new pathway through which these young Negroes could express their pent-up yearning for equality. That they seized on this method with such enthusiasm and courage in the face of possible violence was a sign of their feeling of impotence within the established political system, and an indication of the depth of their frustrations.

The sit-in movement began on February 1, 1960, in Greensboro, North Carolina, when a small group of Negro college students took seats at a lunch counter and refused to leave when told that the store did not serve Negroes. The manager is reported to have said: "They can just sit there. It's nothing to me." But it was something to other Negro college students across the South; within a week similar groups were sitting down in protest all over the region, and a major social movement was underway.

At the beginning there was no central agency engaged in organizing the protests. No such organization was needed. The movement spread spontaneously because the same feelings of impatience and frustration which had moved the Greensboro students to stage their demonstration existed on the campus of every other predominantly Negro college in the South.

At Atlanta University, news of the "sit down" in Greensboro caused considerable excitement and discussion. As early as February 5, a group of students gathered at a drug store near the campus to discuss staging a protest demonstration of their own. Although several students were involved in these initial discussions, the principal instigator seems to have been 24-year-old Lonnie C. King (no relation to Martin Luther King, Jr.), a native of Atlanta and a veteran of three years of military service. He was a successful athlete, had been active in student government, and was generally a very popular

63

member of the student body. When King read of the demonstration in Greensboro, he immediately decided that the same kind of demonstration could be held in Atlanta. The simplicity of this form of protest appealed most to King; the way it dramatized—starkly and obviously—the injustices he resented so deeply. To Lonnie King, the sit-in demonstration seemed an ideal form of symbolic language which could "let the power structure know just how we felt."[1]

The Atlanta students formed a loose organization, and they hoped to stage their initial demonstration on February 12 (Lincoln's birthday), but it was postponed because an insufficient number of students to make an impressive showing had been contacted. When more formal meetings were called on the campus to organize larger groups, the University administration heard of the students' plans for the first time. The Atlanta students had not revealed their plans to the administrators of the University because they were quite suspicious of both the college president and the established Negro leadership in the city. They did consult with some of the younger faculty members and other young adults, but from the beginning of the movement the students were determined to make their own policy. They consulted with adults throughout the controversy over the sit-ins, and they frequently followed the suggestions of their advisers, but the students were always unpredictable, and no adults ever were in a position to dictate to the student leaders. In fact, the students frequently tried to force the adults into action against their will by taking bold action, thus generating public pressure on the established Negro leaders to act in their support. As one young lawyer who worked closely with the student leaders from the beginning of the movement put it: "This was the real magic of the movement. Nobody knew what the students were doing; then we *had* to come to their rescue."

The presidents of the colleges in the Atlanta University Center were not surprised to learn that their students were planning to join the sit-in movement, but they faced with apprehension the prospect of public demonstrations. During meetings in February they decided that they would try to maintain control over the developments, but that they would not try to stop the demonstrations altogether. They made contact with the student leaders, and on February 17, Dr. Benjamin Mays, President of Morehouse College, was able to persuade the student leaders to postpone a demonstration they were planning for February 19 because of the adverse effects it might have on the trial of Martin Luther King, Jr., which was taking place in Montgomery, Alabama, at that time. On February 20, the presidents of the six colleges in the University Center held a formal meeting with the leaders of student government on each campus and discussed the proposed demonstrations. These meetings took place weekly throughout the rest of the school year, and it was at such a meeting on March 2 that Alvin E. Manley, President of Spelman College, proposed to the students that they draw up some kind of document stating their grievances and making their position clear. There was no agreement that this statement of protest was to be an alternative to public demonstrations. It was agreed only that the students' first order of business should be a clear, open statement of their aims and desires. As Dr. Rufus Clement, President of Atlanta University, put it: "We advised them to begin by telling everyone what [they were] crying about."

Nothing could have pleased an idealistic group of students more than to be charged with the responsibility of producing an eloquent statement of protest. The student leaders went to work immediately to draft the document. They found an excellent source of facts concerning the scope of discrimination in the city in a pamphlet entitled *Atlanta: A Second Look* which had been published only two months before. It had been produced under the auspices of the Atlanta Committee for Cooperative Action, a group formed in 1958 by a group of younger men who were becoming dissatisfied with the progress toward equality being made in the city. Essentially, A.C.C.A. was a political club, restricted in membership to men under forty who held liberal or militant views. It was designed as a center for the encouragement of militancy in all the established community organizations, and by the publication of *A Second Look* it was hoped that the magnitude of discrimination in the city could be dramatized. The formation of A.C.C.A. and the appearance of *A Second Look* were indications that the students were not alone in their impatience and resentment at the restrictions of segregation.

The document was ready on March 8 and, after a few minor alterations, it was approved by the college presidents. Money to publish it had already been gathered from the Negro business community; it appeared the following day, March 9, as a full page advertisement in *The Atlanta Constitution, The Atlanta Journal,* and *The Atlanta Daily World* under the title: "An Appeal for Human Rights."

The statement began with a pledge of "unqualified support" for the students participating in sit-in demonstrations in other cities and then stated bluntly:

The students who instigate and participate in these sit-down protests are dissatisfied, not only with the existing conditions, but with the snail-like speed at which they are being ameliorated. Every normal human being wants to walk the earth with dignity and abhors any and all proscriptions placed upon him because of race or color. In essence, this is the meaning of the sit-down protests that are sweeping this nation today. Today's youth will not sit by submissively, while being denied all of the rights, privileges, and joys of life. We want to state clearly and unequivocally that we cannot tolerate, in a nation professing democracy and among people professing Christianity, the discriminatory conditions under which the Negro is living today in Atlanta, Georgia—supposedly one of the most progressive cities in the South.

This declaration was followed by a description of the unequal conditions existing in several areas such as: education, where only four percent of the state's expenditures for higher education were spent on its segregated colleges for Negroes; housing, where Atlanta's Negroes, thirty-two percent of the total population of the city, lived within only sixteen percent of the total area; and health services, where only 680 of the over 4,000 beds in the city's hospitals were available to Negroes. All these statements were based on material found in *Atlanta: A Second Look*.

The Appeal, written in the kind of language which most white people had never heard before from Negroes, ended with a clear promise that further action would be taken:

The time has come for the people of Atlanta and Georgia to take a good look at what is really happening in this country, and to stop believing those who tell us that everything is fine and equal, and that the Negro is happy and satisfied . . . We must say in all candor that we plan to use every legal and non-violent means at our disposal to secure full citizenship rights as members of this great democracy of ours.

This statement provoked public notice and newspaper comment all over the country, and statements concerning it were made by many local public officials. The comments of William Hartsfield, Mayor of Atlanta at the time, and Ernest Vandiver, Governor of Georgia, illustrate dramatically the different political climates that existed in the city and state. The Mayor's statement was short but emphatic. He praised the Appeal and called it "a message of great importance to Atlanta" which expressed "the legitimate aspirations of young people throughout the nation and the entire world." He commended the students for "the promise of non-violence and a peaceful approach." In contrast, the Governor, representing at that time the predominantly rural segments of the state's population, attacked the students and their Appeal by saying:

> I have read the "paid advertisement" purporting to come from students of the six affiliated institutions forming the Atlanta University Center. The statement was skillfully prepared. Obviously it was not written by students. Regrettably, it had the same overtones which are usually found in anti-American propaganda pieces. It did not sound like it was prepared in any Georgia school or college; nor, in fact, did it read like it was written even in this country. This left-wing statement is calculated to breed dissatisfaction, discontent, discord and evil.

The Appeal provoked more than public statements, however, and on the afternoon of March 9, Mayor Hartsfield was in the office of Rufus B. Clement, President of Atlanta University, in order to meet with Lonnie King and the rest of the student leaders responsible for the Appeal. A general exchange of views took place and the Mayor urged them to talk to the city's businessmen before staging any protest demonstrations. He promised to arrange a meeting with prominent members of the Chamber of Commerce so that some of the students' grievances, especially those having to do with segregation in restaurants and employment, might be discussed. Three days later the same student leaders and their college presidents met with a group of the most prominent white ministers in the city, and once again they were given the opportunity to express their feelings. At this meeting the students were urged again to hold up their demonstrations until a meeting could be arranged between them and some of the city's leading businessmen.

King and the other student leaders were not prepared to follow this advice. They were determined to hold at least one protest demonstration to dramatize their appeal, and they wanted to do so before it was forgotten by the community. Their movement was just beginning to gain momentum, and they felt compelled to prove their courage and their militancy by employing "direct action" at least once. Their courage was reinforced by the widespread approval with which their Appeal had been met, and even by the attacks on it (which they considered ludicrous) by the Governor. When they found that the Mayor and prominent white ministers seemed impressed with their arguments, they became increasingly assured of the justice of their cause and even more anxious to stage a public demonstration.

The first sit-ins took place on March 15, six days after the appearance of the Appeal. Approximately 200 students were involved in well-rehearsed protests that occurred at restaurants and lunch counters in the State Capitol building, Fulton County Courthouse, two downtown office buildings used exclusively by agencies of the federal government, all the city's bus and train stations, and the City Hall. The demonstrations were limited to eating facilities located in publicly controlled or tax-supported buildings, and were designed both to create a court case and to dramatize the students' Appeal. The state legislature, anticipating the possibility of sit-in protests in Georgia following the pattern set in North Carolina, on February 17 had passed a new trespass law designed to reinforce the authority of proprietors of eating establishments to have unwanted customers ejected by the police. This law was invoked during the initial sit-in, and seventy-seven students were arrested.

Once again the students had caused a sensation in both the Negro and white communities. Editorial comment from *The Atlanta Constitution* gave cautious support to demonstrations designed solely to establish a test case. But the paper emphasized the danger of the explosion of violence in the wake of such public displays of discontent and declared:

> The processes of law have been started. These can he handled without any public interference by agitators bent on disorder. We are a nation which must continue to live by law and this is a good time to remember it. We all have too much at stake in the present and future of this city to besmirch it with violence or extreme action. Let none of us forget that important fact.

The first sit-in did not receive unanimous approval from the Negro community. The Negro-owned *Atlanta Daily World*, which had been advising against the use of demonstrations since the first sit-in in Greensboro, withheld its full support. Mr C. A. Scott, publisher and editor of the *Daily World*, questioned in his editorial the "necessity here in Atlanta to continue the demonstrations," and advised the students to use their energies to pass a "meaningful civil rights law," or to "join in this campaign to get every eligible Negro registered to vote." He asserted:

> There are many problems to be resolved, but some are more important than others. We give high priority to these questions: the elimination of segregation in education, more voting and political influence, equal consideration in the administration of justice at the state level and improved economic opportunities.

Two prominent Negro lawyers, D. L. Hollowell and A. T. Walden, left immediately for New York to attend a conference on the legal questions raised by the sit-ins, which was organized by the NAACP. Both men expressed support for the demonstrations and praised the students, but they also implied that since a legal issue had been raised further demonstrations would be unnecessary. Dr. Rufus Clement expressed a hope that there would be no more demonstrations and added that the students "feel much better now that they have stated their beliefs and dramatized them, but I think they still strongly feel that something should be done about their Appeal." The typical reaction of most adult Negro leaders at this time seemed to be a mixture of caution and warm praise as expressed by the Reverend William Holmes Borders when he told a meeting of the students: "I don't think you need to do it again soon, but thank God you did it yesterday!"

The students were unclear about what their next move should be. They were suspicious of both the white and Negro leaders involved, and they were afraid that if they left the issue to be decided by the courts it would take a long time, and the danger was great that nothing would ever be done. They decided to form an organization to continue some sort of protest activity, and on March 16, 1960, The Committee on an Appeal for Human Rights was created with Lonnie King as chairman. The first act of the committee was to issue a public statement that no further public demonstrations were planned. The statement also included a further appeal addressed, rather vaguely, to "whatever delegation that wants to talk to us," which said:

> Yesterday's requests for services were made at eating establishments operating on tax supported premises. This was another step toward the fulfillment of the aim of our "Appeal for Human Rights." On the basis of that appeal, we would welcome the opportunity for further discussion leading to its implementation.

This request was not completely disregarded. Even before the first sit-ins, the ministerial group with which the student leaders had met earlier had been working to arrange a meeting for the students with some of the city's leading businessmen. They had hoped that a direct exchange of views in a face-to-face meeting might increase understanding between the two groups, and they had hoped that such exchanges might even lead to the peaceful negotiation of some of the students' grievances. These hopes were dashed, however, by the results of the meeting which took place a few days after the first sit-in. The business leaders listened to the students in silence and then criticized the contents of their Appeal. One man took the same attitude expressed earlier by the Governor and is reported to have said that it "smacked of Communism"; another very influential white business leader is reported to have bluntly told the students that he was "not even thinking about thinking about doing away with segregation!" The students left this meeting shocked by the hostility they had encountered, and as a result of this confrontation, they became more convinced that continued protest action was necessary.

Mayor Hartsfield was as much convinced that he must make an effort to stop any further demonstrations by the students. To press his point, he made an appearance before the Hungry Club, a luncheon club of Negro leaders which met weekly at the Butler Street YMCA. Over the years, this club had become the best forum in the city from which a white leader could address the Negro community. In his talk, the Mayor argued that boycotts and demonstrations should not be used to gain equality because they hurt "business and innocent merchants." He advised an increased campaign of education through television and more newspaper advertisements: "You must educate the public about the position of the Negro today. Above all else, educate the white man . . . Most of your trouble comes from the uneducated." He also reminded them that violence could erupt as a result of the protests and warned them that "when you demonstrate, you are taking a terrible chance, because you are no longer in a position of controlling what happens." He concluded by asking them to be considerate of the difficulties of "white moderates" like himself who bore a heavy cross because of their opinions. He warned them that they could not win their fight without support from "the better elements" of the white people: "Respectable white people will support you, so long as your conduct merits it."

Only a few days after the Mayor made his appeal for an end to demonstrations, during the first week in April, several student leaders, including Lonnie King, James Gibson, Julian Bond, and others, began consulting a group of young adult leaders, including Carl Holman, a young professor at Clark College; Leroy Johnson, an attorney; and Jessie Hill, an executive with Atlanta Life Insurance Company, all of whom were active members of the Atlanta Committee for Cooperative Action. The purpose of their meetings was to discuss the next moves in the protest movement. The student leaders were determined at this point to demonstrate further; the only question for discussion was where and how. The young adult leaders felt that they would be more successful if they concentrated on small merchants or stores with large Negro clienteles which did not hire Negroes above the menial level. The students feared that if they followed that course and sought only limited objectives they would not be able to marshall the enthusiasm necessary to maintain a large number of active workers. They were convinced that an overwhelming majority of the students supported their actions, but they had found that it was very difficult to rouse large numbers into action. The students decided to follow the advice of the adults at this time, but they were uneasy and still felt that it was important to create a major issue if possible.

An Atlantic & Pacific supermarket was selected as the first target for direct action in this new phase of the students' campaign. It had a predominantly Negro clientele but did not hire Negroes above the most menial levels. The student leaders made efforts between April 16 and April 22 through letters and a series of telephone conversations to set up negotiations with the management of A & P to promote some Negroes and to hire others in more skilled capacities, They had two meetings with A & P officials, but each time only the company's employment policies were explained, and no offer was made to change them. On April 22 picket lines were set up around the A & P store, and a boycott was declared.

Although the boycott was generally effective, this action immediately produced strong criticisms from within the Negro community. The *Daily World*, which lost A & P's advertising as a result of the picketing, complained that the public had not been informed of any efforts to negotiate the difficulties and asked who made the decision to start picketing. It called for the formation of a community-wide organization to plan future actions and added: "We firmly believe there should be a sincere effort at negotiation to satisfy not only the employment issue but any other question before resorting to drastic picketing."

Mr. C. A. Scott, the editor of the *Daily World*, made personal efforts to arrange more meetings between the students and the store managers and called repeatedly for conciliatory action. Meetings were held in early May between student leaders and A & P officials, but they were fruitless. The management of A & P refused to recognize Lonnie King and the other members of the Committee on an Appeal for Human Rights as legitimate bargaining agents; they were determined not to give in to the boycott even if they were forced to operate their store at a loss indefinitely.

As a result of its clash with A & P, several older, conservative Negro leaders began openly criticizing the students' activities at public meetings. The *Daily World* refused to publish pictures of Negroes who began to cross the picket line to patronize the supermarket, and it also attacked the students' adult advisers: "in the present controversy, there is serious question as to whether the adult advisers cautioned or urged the proper exhaustion of other remedies before resorting to picketing." The student leaders grew very angry at this criticism and seriously considered picketing the offices of the *Daily World* in protest against the attitudes of its editor. They were dissuaded from this action by their adult advisers, but they became convinced during this period that their movement needed to be strengthened by a bigger, more dramatic demonstration of protest.

The opportunity to stage such a demonstration presented itself on May 17, the sixth anniversary of the Supreme Court's decision that segregation in the public schools was unconstitutional. The student leaders decided to organize a protest march from the campus of Atlanta University to the grounds of the State Capitol to commemorate that day. Preparations went forward secretly, and on Sunday, May 15, at a meeting of the representatives of NAACP chapters from all over the southeast, they made a dramatic announcement of their plans.

On Monday the impending march made front page news and caused excitement throughout the city. Governor Vandiver issued a sharp warning that he would not allow the marchers on the Capitol grounds and said that "appropriate" preventive action would be taken. In contrast the Mayor called for calmness and said:

> We are veterans of marches and demonstrations by both whites and Negroes. When the White Citizen Councils threatened a march last year, we suggested they schedule it to correspond with the Southeastern Fair dates. It is none of my business, probably, but if I were governor, I would invite them inside [the Capitol] to see that wonderful museum.

On Tuesday morning, however, state highway patrolmen, armed with nightsticks, fire hoses, and tear gas, were deployed around the State Capitol building, and a large, angry crowd of whites was gathering to meet the demonstrators. The Mayor called officials at Atlanta University and asked them to stop the demonstrations because he was afraid that a race riot was imminent. The college officials were extremely reluctant to order the students not to carry out a peaceful demonstration, but Dr. Benjamin Mays did issue a brief statement during the morning which said: "in the light of public excitement, it would be wise if the students did not demonstrate downtown today." This was not enough to dissuade them, however, and early in the afternoon over 2,000 students with the officers of the Committee on an

Appeal for Human Rights in the lead, left the campus for the walk of over a mile to the Capitol building in downtown Atlanta.

A few blocks from the Capitol the leaders of the marchers were confronted by Atlanta's Chief of Police Herbert Jenkins. After looking over the crowd at the Capitol, he had decided that a riot would be unavoidable if the students continued, so he ordered the marchers to proceed to a large Negro church near the Capitol. Lonnie King and the other student leaders hesitated, and the officer repeated his order; then without comment they altered their route. A group of about 400 students at the end of the line who had become separated from the main body did actually walk by the Capitol while the crowd watched and shouted insults, but this group also turned away from the grounds and marched to the church where the demonstration ended peacefully with prayers, songs, and speeches. As if to top off the day, a smaller group of students staged a sit-in during the evening at the city auditorium where a musical comedy was being performed before a segregated audience.

This eventful day served to raise racial tensions in the city considerably. On May 18, Governor Vandiver threateningly announced that he was having the state Attorney General investigate the tax-exempt status of Atlanta's private Negro colleges. Within the Negro community, arguments over the wisdom of protest demonstrations raged both privately and publicly. For example, at a public meeting on May 23 (organized to raise money for legal defense in the sit-in cases) the president of the local chapter of the NAACP, The Reverend Samuel Williams, attacked those adults who did not support the students. He pledged his organization's full backing and charged that those who opposed the sit-ins were either "Victims of brain washing or profiting from a system." He also urged the students to "continue this fight. You are entitled to everything you are asking for." And a student speaker, Benjamin Brown, drew thunderous applause when he shouted: "A certain Negro newspaper is trying to hamper our cause. But we're here to say no single newspaper is going to stop us!"

The increasing disunity among adult Negroes, caused by the disagreements over the student movement, prompted several people to endorse the suggestion made in March by the *Daily World* that some kind of communitywide organization be formed to advise the students and unite the various factions in the city's Negro civic leadership. A meeting was called on May 26 by a group of both liberal and conservative leaders, and such an organization, called the Student-Adult Liaison Committee, was formed on

June 2. At this meeting a subcommittee was appointed to draw up a statement endorsing the student movement and emphasizing the unity of the Negro community. This statement, signed by the officers of all the community-wide voluntary Negro civic organizations in the city, appeared as a one-third page advertisement in all of the city's daily newspapers on May 30, and stated in part:

> We take this opportunity to commend the students for their courage and for the pattern of orderly, peaceful and non-violent behavior that has characterized all of their activities. We endorse the objectives stated in the students' "Appeal for Human Rights," and we also endorse efforts of the student movement to secure increased employment opportunities for qualified Negroes.

The organizers of the Student-Adult Liaison Committee were successful in bringing together all the Negro civic organizations in the city, but some influential figures in the community, including such men as C. A. Scott, editor and publisher of the *Daily World*, were still highly skeptical and distrustful of the students' efforts. That such lingering opposition existed was admitted by a spokesman for the Student-Adult Liaison Committee when he was questioned about the advertisement by reporters. When asked why the advertisement had been put into the newspapers he said:

> There had been some talk that the adult Negroes—particularly those who might be classed as well off—did not support the young people's action. This advertisement should prove that there is no basis of fact for such statements. Of course, there are some individuals who don't agree with their stand or ours, but every organization the committee approached gave its wholehearted support to the advertisement.

With the coming of the summer recess most of the students at Atlanta University left the city, but the leaders of the Committee on an Appeal for Human Rights remained in town and began a vigorous effort to build support for their movement in the Negro community. The students devised a program called "The Student Movement and You" which was presented throughout the summer before numerous church and civic groups; they were able to convince two radio stations which direct their programs to Atlanta's Negro community to schedule weekly news shows on the student movement, and they began publishing a weekly information sheet in leaflet form.

Besides these efforts to increase community understanding and support, the student leaders also made a decision to resume sit-in demonstrations. But instead of limiting their efforts to restaurants in public buildings, they decided to sit-in at Rich's, Inc., the largest downtown department store. This change in strategy took place because the student leaders became convinced that the desegregation of all eating facilities was within their power. By the summer, approximately sixty cities in the upper South and Southwest had desegregated private facilities, and the students became determined to achieve no less in Atlanta.

Rich's was chosen as a target because it was the dominant retail institution in town, and because it was locally owned. In April, the adult advisers of the students had argued against attacking Rich's because it had "deep roots in the community." It had been the first major store in the city to extend credit to Negroes, and it had also been the first to instruct its sales personnel to address all Negro customers as "Mr." and "Mrs." Segregated drinking fountains had quietly been removed some years before, and the store employed large numbers of Negroes, although not in sales, white collar, or managerial capacities. Mr. Richard Rich, the president of the company, was considered to be a liberal community leader, and he had a record of supporting the established Negro leadership in several controversies over housing and welfare. By attacking an institution with such a reputation for liberalism, the students placed the city's established Negro leadership in very awkward circumstances.

On the afternoon of June 24, Lonnie King and several other student leaders were quietly picked up by the city police and brought downtown where they had a personal confrontation with Mr. Rich at the central police station. Mr. Rich arranged this meeting so that he could review the history of his store and its liberal accomplishments. He told the students that because he was Jewish he understood discrimination and had great sympathy for their aspirations; but he also argued that their protest demonstrations were dangerous and should be stopped. In exchange for an end to the sit-ins in his store, he promised that after the schools were peacefully desegregated he would personally call all the city's merchants together to try to bring a peaceful end to segregation in lunch counters and restaurants. The students rejected this suggestion and asserted that they were not prepared to wait any longer to get what they were morally entitled to have immediately. They called his proposals "a lot of Uncle Tom business" and told him that if he did not agree to desegregate they would organize a boycott against him. As far as they were concerned, he had treated Negroes with more dignity in his store only to gain their business, and one student is reported to have said: "This is a revolution. We aren't waiting any longer." These replies greatly shocked Mr. Rich, and he asserted that he could get along without Negro trade at his store. He told the students that he would never yield before threats and intimidation and angrily left the room.

Three days later, on June 27, a small group of students attempted a sit-in at Rich's once again, and on the next day a circular was issued by the Committee on an Appeal for Human Rights calling for a boycott of the store by Negroes. This move made it clear that the students were planning to mount a determined campaign to gain their objectives, and the *Journal*, the *Constitution*, and the *Daily World* all replied with editorials attacking "pressure tactics."

Within the Negro community, arguments over the student movement were becoming more intense. The students decided in mid-July that they should try to establish a weekly newspaper which would support their movement, and they were successful in persuading the association of Negro real estate agents, the Empire Real Estate Board, to take its advertising out of the *Daily World* and place it exclusively in a new weekly to be called *The Atlanta Inquirer* which published its first issue on July 31. In a letter to C. A. Scott, editor of the *Daily World*, Joseph T. Bickers, president of the real-estate board, said:

> . . . our membership feels strongly that financial support to any organization or individual who fails to take advantage of opportunities to promote the cause sponsored by these young people is detrimental to the best interests of our people.

Mr. Scott, however, was not without allies within the Negro community at this period. Four days after the decision by the real-estate board, Warren Cochrane, executive secretary of the Butler Street YMCA and secretary of the Atlanta Negro Voters League, attacked the methods of the student movement in a public speech. He deplored the concentration on Rich's which he described as "an institution which has been a household word in the Atlanta community, an institution which has dealt generously with the Negro community in both employment and courtesy," and he also argued that:

The race must keep all of the friends it has in the dominant white world and work unceasingly to multiply them. Potent will be that discriminating intelligence by which Negroes will acknowledge the blessings they enjoy as well as the wrongs they suffer.

During the month of August, the students discontinued their sit-ins at Rich's, but they organized a series of "kneel-ins" at white churches, and they doggedly maintained their picket line in front of the A & P supermarket. This picket line was joined on one day by several Negro physicians and on another day by their wives, but it was becoming increasingly ineffective, and a decision was made during the last week in August to abandon it altogether. At the same time, a reconciliation of sorts took place between the real estate board and the *Daily World*, and as a result, real estate notices began appearing in both the *Daily World* and the *Inquirer*.

Early in September, efforts were made to begin negotiations with Colonial Stores, Inc., a regional chain, to change its employment policies at another supermarket in the Negro community. After fruitless talks a picket line was set up on September 3, and again it was initially extremely effective in keeping Negro customers out of the store. Two-and-one-half weeks later, on September 23, the store was closed. It reopened on September 30, with newly hired Negro clerks and other Negroes promoted from menial jobs.[2] The elated student leaders immediately approached a smaller supermarket on that day with similar demands, and had a satisfactory agreement after only an hour's negotiation. With these triumphs fresh in their minds they held a mass meeting the next day on the Atlanta University campus designed to "initiate" the returning college students into the movement.

The stage was now set for the Committee on an Appeal for Human Rights' "fall campaign." During the summer, extensive plans had been made for large scale sit-in demonstrations beginning on October 7 accompanied by a boycott of the entire downtown area by all Negroes. It was impossible to organize the demonstrations so early, but twelve days later preparations were completed. On October 19, the city's newspapers carried banner headlines announcing large-scale sit-ins at Rich's and seven other downtown department and variety stores. To further single out Rich's, picket lines were set up around the store and renewed pleas were made by all student leaders for a complete boycott of the downtown area. One reporter wrote that the protests were "as coordinated as military maneuvers on a drill field." The fall campaign was underway.

From the beginning of the fall demonstrations, the trespass law was invoked by the merchants, and on the first day Lonnie King and several other student leaders, along with Martin Luther King, were arrested. The student leaders had initiated and planned the demonstrations; Martin Luther King was persuaded to participate only the night before. Although the national press focused great attention on him, he was not the leader of these demonstrations. His policy was to remain aloof from the Atlanta situation, where so many skilled Negro leaders existed, and concentrate his own attention on other areas which were in greater need of organization and leadership. But Atlanta was his home and Morehouse College, a part of Atlanta University, was his alma mater. The students urged him to help them and at the last minute he agreed. Later he explained that he participated "because the students asked me to come and I felt a moral responsibility to join them."

Some merchants responded to the sit-in demonstrators by turning off the lights in their lunch counters and closing temporarily, but the Negro students sat silently on in the dark. On October 20, even more demonstrators appeared and protests were staged at eleven, instead of only eight, stores. The total of those arrested rose to fifty-seven students, all of whom vowed to stay in jail without attempting to post bond.

During the next day picketing continued, but the number of sit-ins declined. At this point, the Mayor began making efforts to bring an end to the demonstrations and get negotiations started. He contacted several adult Negro leaders and asked for a "truce" of at least sixty days during which the sit-ins would cease. He received such assurances from the adult leaders, but he had not contacted the student leaders directly, and when he made a public statement that he had arranged a temporary halt in the protests, a student spokesman immediately issued a denial and indignantly called the Mayor's statement "absolutely unauthentic." He asserted that: "The Mayor has talked to no student leaders. He cannot speak for us."

On the next day, however, after the students had been contacted, the sit-ins were halted, and the Mayor held a meeting with all sixty members of the Student-Adult Liaison Committee in the City Hall. After a meeting which lasted almost three hours, the Mayor announced that the demonstrations would cease for a period of thirty days beginning on October 23. During this time the Mayor promised to contact the downtown merchants and try to arrive at a peaceful settlement of the dispute. The fifty-seven demonstrators who had been arrested, including Martin Luther King, Jr.,[3] were to be released and there were to be no protests of any kind during this period.

During the month that followed several efforts were made to reach a negotiated settlement of the dispute, but all of them were unsuccessful. The Mayor was able to persuade many of the smaller downtown merchants who feared the consequences of a Negro boycott to consider desegregation, but he was unable to get a representative of Rich's even to attend negotiating sessions with him. The management of this dominant store was in no mood to negotiate an immediate settlement at this time, and they were also suspicious of the Mayor whose political strength depended on maintaining Negro votes. As one member of the store's management put it: "We just weren't prepared to involve our store in politics."

While rejecting the Mayor's overtures, however, the management of Rich's was initiating informal efforts of their own designed to bring the boycott and sit-ins to an end. Two of the best-established Negro leaders, one a successful businessman and the other a distinguished educator, were asked to come to Rich's to discuss the sit-in problem during the second week in November. At this first meeting, which was kept secret, the desire of Rich's management to have the protest ended was explained and the two leaders were asked to suggest the names of other leaders who might be willing to discuss the issue and help bring the disturbances to an end. A few days later a larger group, made up once again of older, established Negro leaders, was secretly assembled at Rich's. The store's management repeated essentially the same proposal made by Mr. Rich to the student leaders during the summer. They asked that the protests be called off until after the schools were desegregated, at which time they would promise to call all the downtown merchants together and try to arrive at a peaceful solution of the problem of segregated lunch counters. The meeting was not meant to be a negotiating session. The proposals of the company were discussed, however, and it was decided that another meeting should be held at which actual negotiation would take place, this time including an adult leader from the more liberal group and the most outstanding student leader.

While these plans were being made, the Mayor's period of truce was coming to an end. He had been giving weekly reports of his progress to the leaders of the Student-Adult Liaison Committee and on November 23, he had to report to then that he had been unable even to assemble all the merchants, and that no settlement had been reached. The Mayor asked for an extension of thirty days in the truce period, but he was granted only three

79

more days extending through the Thanksgiving holiday. At this meeting, the Mayor was upset and quite critical of the merchants. One Negro leader said: "We were pretty sure he didn't really want an extension of time. He just felt he had to ask for it as a negotiator. I'm sure we did him a favor by giving him only three days."

When it became clear that the Mayor's efforts were going to be fruitless, Cecil Alexander, a young white architect, made an effort to act as a mediator in the conflict. He had always been interested in the political life of the city and was an active supporter of Mayor Hartsfield; he had worked closely with several Negro leaders on citizens' committees dealing with the city's urban renewal program; he was related by marriage to high officials at Rich's, and was trusted by Mr. Rich. Due to these personal qualifications he was successful in assembling a representative group of Negro and white leaders to discuss the deadlock and search for a compromise. In order to keep the meeting secret and to find a time when every one could attend, it was scheduled to take place at Alexander's office at midnight on Thanksgiving, November 24.

The group that assembled included leading Negro businessmen; the officers of the Student-Adult Liaison Committee; Dr. Benjamin Mays, President of Morehouse College; Martin Luther King, Jr. ; student leaders, including Lonnie King; and Mr. Rich. The meeting was informal, and there was no agenda. It was designed simply as an exchange of views, and it soon turned into a rambling discussion of the status of the dispute and the issues at stake. Mr. Rich argued once again that the integration of the schools, which was expected to begin one year later in the fall of 1961, was the city's most important problem. He was afraid that to desegregate the lunch counters at this time would unduly excite racial fears and passions, and jeopardize the success of this crucial undertaking.

The Negro leaders argued in reply that the students, by their repeated protest demonstrations, had radically increased the importance of segregation in lunch counters and restaurants, and had created a major problem that should be immediately solved. They pointed out that tensions existed at that time in the city that might lead to explosive violence long before autumn. Mr. Rich was urged to take steps at once to remove the barriers of segregation at the lunch counters and restaurants in his store in order to ease these dangerous tensions and to prove that desegregation would work. Rich rejected this argument, however, asserting that segregation was a public policy and should be dealt with first in public, not private institutions. He held that his department store, a private institution, should not be forced to become the "bellwether of change."

Even though he refused to agree to immediate desegregation, Rich did repeat his promise to bring the merchants together and try to work out a settlement after the school desegregation crisis was past. He also promised to look into the employment policies of his store. The meeting ended inconclusively, but Mr. Alexander felt that at least a basis for further discussion and negotiation had been established. But Lonnie King, Herschelle Sullivan, Benjamin Brown, and the other student leaders were not willing to suspend their demonstrations any longer. Nothing concrete had yet been won. They still had only promises and vague assurances that sincere efforts would be made sometime in the future to do away with segregation at the lunch counters. They feared that to settle for such a meager victory after so much effort had been extended might permanently undermine and discredit their movement. There was also a lingering suspicion in their minds that this was only an effort to keep them from disrupting Rich's annual post-Thanksgiving sale. On the next day the students announced that they were resuming their protests. In a public statement they said:

> We intend to do it for as long as it takes. It has never been our intention to hurt our city, the merchants or anyone else. We do want, however, to remove the hurt from the hearts of Negroes who've been hurting for over one hundred years.

The resumption of picketing did not end the efforts to negotiate an agreement to end the dispute. It had been agreed at the secret November meetings between the management of Rich's and the older, established Negro leaders that another meeting should take place. This time, the conference was to include a student leader and one young adult, and efforts would be made to negotiate an end to the protest demonstrations. It was decided that this meeting should be held on Monday, November 28, even though the students had resumed their picketing in the downtown area. The meeting was to have been secret, and its sponsors had high hopes that meaningful negotiations could take place. On Sunday, however, news of the planned meeting leaked out when one of the older Negro leaders, who knew of the plans but disapproved of them, dropped hints to a reporter that an important meeting was being planned. The two younger leaders invited to the secret meeting were Lonnie King, chairman of the Committee on an Appeal for Human Rights, and Jessie Hill, an insurance executive who was an active member of the Atlanta Committee for Cooperative Action and who had been an adviser of the students from the beginning of the protest movement. Once these two found that they were to be the only representatives of those who had been actively engaged in the protests, they became very suspicious of the purpose of the meeting. After consulting other students and younger adults they decided that they would not cooperate in this venture. They publicly announced their refusal to attend, and they said that any future negotiations would be unsuccessful unless it included all those who were involved in conducting the protest demonstrations. The representatives of Rich's and the older Negro leaders arrived at the meeting place unaware that their plans had been made public, and were confronted with television cameras and reporters clamoring for statements.

After this abortive effort at negotiation, tension rose between the two races in the city. Many Negro adults appeared on the picket lines to express their sympathy with the students, and the Ku Klux Klan, in full uniform, began picketing the Negro student pickets. Lunch counters in most of the downtown stores were closed permanently, and the students used a radio-equipped automobile to bring sit-in demonstrators immediately to any store which opened its facilities. The boycott of the downtown area called for by the students was extremely effective. In response, an extreme segregationist organization called "Georgians Unwilling to Surrender" (GUTS) threatened to organize a counter-boycott against all downtown stores which hired Negroes, and a letter from the Student-Adult Liaison Committee requesting negotiating meetings with the merchants received a completely negative response. The Mayor could report no progress in finding a solution to the dispute, but he did add a note of humor to an otherwise grim situation by saying:

> Well, at least in the field of lunch counter demonstrations, Atlanta can claim two firsts. With the help of the Ku Klux Klan, it can be the first to claim integrated picketing. And now we have radio-directed picketing. At least we are handling our problems in a progressive way.

The number of whites heckling the student pickets was increasing during the first week of December, and the level of tension was rising. The combination of the boycott by the Negroes, the possibility of violence, and the inconvenience caused to customers because of the closed lunch counters was producing a decline in retail business at downtown stores.

The Negroes gave impressive testimony to their determination on Sunday, December 11, when over 2,500 attended a sunrise prayer meeting sponsored by the Student-Adult Liaison Committee. They met at a football stadium in the Negro community in a chilling rain, and then marched almost two miles into the downtown area where another prayer meeting was held in a small park in the center of the city.

Attitudes on both sides seemed to be hardening, and the threat of racial violence, which had been present since the demonstrations began, now hung ominously over the city. At 2:20 A.M. December 12 the threat materialized when a bomb exploded at a Negro elementary school shattering hundreds of windows throughout the neighborhood, damaging the school considerably, and blowing a four foot hole in the sidewalk. The city was shocked; both civic and religious leaders deplored the incident. Mayor Hartsfield spoke out very strongly:

> Such senseless destruction of property is the work of the lowest element, an ignorant rabble, inflamed by political demagogues and encouraged by the silence of our substantial civic leaders. Practically all the rabble-rousing, cross-burning, sheet-flapping, and dynamiting is done by people who do not live inside the limit of Atlanta . . . the out-house crowd . . . Incidentally, it is time for the substantial citizens of Atlanta—the people who own its great stores, office buildings, plants and factories—to assert themselves. Otherwise a few little, loud-mouthed racial demagogues will be mistaken for the voice of Atlanta.

In the wake of this outbreak of violence and the strong statement by the Mayor, the Student-Adult Liaison Committee called on the Retail Merchants Association, the Atlanta Chamber of Commerce and the Junior Chamber of Commerce to meet with them to begin negotiations for a settlement of the dispute. All three groups refused to meet with the Negro leaders but called on them to bring their demonstrations and boycotts to an end.

The remainder of December and all of January passed with the community in a stalemate. The Negroes' boycott remained effective but with final examinations approaching the students reduced their picketing to Fridays and Saturdays. There were occasional sit-ins at lunch counters which tried to reopen, and both the student demonstrators and the merchants seemed determined to maintain their positions. Toward the end of January the attention of the whole state switched from Atlanta to Athens, Georgia, the site of the State University, where two Negro students were successfully enrolled after two days of rioting by white students. The state legislature, now faced directly with the prospect of either yielding or closing the state's schools, dramatically decided to accept the inevitable and leave the University open. At the urging of the Governor they voted to repeal Georgia's so-called "massive resistance" statutes and a major crisis was averted.

With the beginning of the second semester the student leaders decided to make a more determined effort in the downtown area. On February 1, the anniversary of the initial Greensboro sit-in, several hundred students marched downtown and set up picket lines around all the major downtown department and variety stores. The president of Atlanta University is reported to have cautioned the student leaders, suggesting that they seek to negotiate their dispute, but he did not try to stop them from demonstrating.

On February 7, during a sit-in at a restaurant in an office building leased exclusively by agencies of the federal government, an argument broke out between Lonnie King and the manager which resulted in the arrest of seventeen students under the Georgia trespass law. The students had not planned to get arrested, and this development caught them by surprise. After consultation, it was decided to press the issue; the next day another group returned to the same restaurant and thirteen more students were arrested. Both sides lost their patience at this point, and the students resolved not to make bond but to crowd the jails in protest. Arrests now began taking place all over town, and by February 11, over eighty students were behind bars.

The resumption of arrests once again provoked from conservative Negroes criticism of the students' methods, and rumors spread through the white community that the students were losing the support of the adult leaders. Reports of the students in jail were no longer front page news in the *Journal* or *Constitution*, and the merchants still refused to negotiate with the Student-Adult Liaison Committee. Some of the students in the jails became restless and wondered if they would lose a complete semester of college if they remained much longer. The possibility grew that the protest movement might suffer a major setback that could dramatically undermine its community support.

In order to demonstrate support for the students, a mass meeting was called on February 15 at which Martin Luther King was the principal speaker. A protest march and rally in front of the county jail to dramatize the students' efforts was planned for February 19, the following Sunday, and The Reverend Samuel Williams, expressing the mood of almost desperate determination felt by some Negro leaders at that time, told the audience: "We're going to stay with, and even *die* with the students if necessary!"

Following this mass meeting, a small group of Negro leaders gathered to discuss the state of affairs. Included among this group was Lonnie King, Benjamin Brown, and other student leaders; Leroy Johnson, Carl Holman, Jessie Hill, the most militant young adults, The Reverend William Holmes Borders, chairman of the Student-Adult Liaison Committee; and A. T. Walden, a highly respected attorney and political leader. At this tense meeting, Walden, who was over seventy years of age and generally considered to be conservative, especially by the students, made a plea that he be given the opportunity to get negotiations started once again. He asked for thirty days, the same length of time granted to the Mayor in October, and he is reported to have made a dramatic pledge that if he failed in this effort he would "take up a sign and march with you in your movement."

Walden's record during the dispute had been rather ambiguous. He had expressed support for the initial sit-in demonstrations, and he was mentioned as one of the attorneys planning to defend the students in the sit-in cases. But he had not continued his praise of the students after it became clear that they were determined to press their demands through continued demonstrations and that they were not planning to rely only on the courts to settle the dispute. He had a long record of community service and had been an important political figure for over twenty years. Walden's name was almost automatically included each time Negro community leaders were called together for almost any reason. He had been invited to both the Thanksgiving night negotiating session in Cecil Alexander's office and the secret meeting at Rich's in November. Although basically conservative in his approach to race relations, he had the respect of several liberal leaders. In fact, on January 7, 1961, Carl Holman, adviser to the student leaders and active member of the Atlanta Committee for Cooperative Action, wrote an editorial in the *Inquirer*, entitled "The Old Campaigner," in which he praised Walden's record. The editorial was written in direct response to criticisms of Walden being made privately at that time by student leaders. They were reminded that:

> It might lend some perspective on the very real risks and the very great courage involved in the early career of A. T. Walden to consider how much harsher then was the opposition to the NAACP than today's daring young sit-in pioneers are faced with.

There was considerable confusion about what was decided at the meeting at which Walden was formally granted permission to act as a bargaining agent for the protest movement. Walden clearly received a mandate to start negotiations if he could, but there was uncertainty over whether he was authorized actually to formulate an agreement or simply to arrange for the talks between the protest leaders and the whites. It was also undecided if demonstrations were to stop while he made his effort. Even after this meeting the students remained in jail, and plans for the protest march in front of the jail went forward.

Apprehension grew over the Negroes' proposed march as the Ku Klux Klan announced it would stage a counter rally at the jail on the same day, and the inmates became very restless. The Mayor called the planned march "a grave mistake" and urged that it be canceled, as did the chief jailer, the county sheriff, and the city police chief. Once again the student leaders were being asked to discontinue their protests and jeopardize the future of their movement without any concrete assurance that desegregation would occur. This time, however, they yielded. After considerable hesitation, on Saturday, February 18, it was decided that the rally would be held at a large downtown Negro church instead of the jail, and several observers expressed the belief that a potential race riot had been averted. Miss Herschelle Sullivan, speaking for the student leaders later at the rally, explained that the students had wanted to march on the jail but had "yielded to wiser judgment" and consented to the alteration in the plans.

Tension was still high in the city, however, and on Monday eight Negro physicians attending a graduate medical assembly at a downtown hotel were arrested when they tried to get food in a segregated cafeteria. On Tuesday, a lone Negro minister was arrested when he entered a segregated cafeteria at one of the city's railroad stations. On Wednesday, however, eight students posted bond and left their cells, and the next day, February 23, all the rest followed their example. The reason given for this action was that firm negotiations seemed possible, and A. T. Walden made a public statement saying that: "The students shall henceforth walk arm and arm with their elders in a supplemental strategy which has been developed by the composite counsel and judgment of youth and age."

By this time, Walden was making progress in getting negotiations underway. He had gone first to see Robert Troutman, Sr., a prominent white attorney who had business connections with Rich's, Inc. Walden and Troutman had never had any direct business dealings with each other, but they had worked together on various charitable fund raising projects during the previous twenty years, and Troutman had been a consistent contributor to various institutions, such as the YMCA and the Urban League, within the Negro community. Troutman advised Walden to try to take the pressure of decision off Rich's and shift it to the whole white business community. He suggested that Walden contact Ivan Allen, Jr., the president of the Atlanta Chamber of Commerce at the time, and try to convince him to work for a solution through the Chamber.

Walden secured an appointment with Allen, with Troutman's help, and after two conferences Allen agreed to make an effort to arrange a settlement of the dispute. Allen contacted the white merchants principally involved in the dispute and together they developed the outline of a compromise settlement that they would be willing to accept. These provisional terms were then presented to Walden who approved them as a basis for discussion. At this point a meeting of the leading merchants and the leaders of the Student-Adult Liaison Committee was arranged at which an effort would be made to reach a final agreement.

The student leaders at this meeting, Lonnie King and Miss Hersehelle Sullivan, were prepared to argue for immediate desegregation of the lunch counters, but they found that the merchants were still unwilling to accept this demand. After considerable persuasion from all the adult leaders present, the student leaders accepted, as a substitute for immediate desegregation, a firm pledge from the merchants that the lunch counters and restroom facilities in their stores would be desegregated sometime after the schools were desegregated the following fall, but no later than October 15, 1961. It was also agreed that the lunch counters and restaurants would be desegregated regardless of what happened to the schools. In exchange for these pledges, Negro leaders agreed that the boycott and the demonstrations would stop immediately, and that all eating facilities could open on a segregated basis. All the employees who had been laid off when the eating facilities had been closed (the overwhelming majority of whom were Negroes) were to be rehired. In this form, except for the firm pledge that the counters would be desegregated and the understanding that desegregation would take place regardless of what happened in the school crisis, the agreement was very nearly what the management of Rich's had been urging since June, 1960.

The agreement was accepted by all sides late Sunday night, March 6, and a public announcement was made on Monday by Ivan Allen in the name of the Chamber of Commerce. It was warmly praised by all the city's daily newspapers. Mayor Hartsfield, in expressing his approval of what had been

87

decided, coined a phrase that was to become the city's semi-official motto during the tense school desegregation of the following fall. He said the agreement proved that: "This is a city too busy to hate."

But within the Negro community the agreement was not greeted with such enthusiasm and pride; in fact, it set off a stormy controversy. In announcing the agreement it had been decided at the Sunday night meeting that no mention of the date, or even of the existence of a deadline, would be made. It was feared that to do otherwise would alert white extremist groups and possibly provoke violent organized protests on the day of the formal desegregation. But when the public announcement of the agreement was made without mention of a specific date, along with word of the reopening of the lunch counters on a segregated basis, it struck the Atlanta Negro community, to quote Carl Holman's editorial in the *Inquirer*, "like a bucket of cold water in the face."

As soon as the agreement was announced, telephones rang all over the city, and those who had been parties to the agreement were the objects of ugly, abusive insults and charges that they had "sold out" to the white merchants. On Wednesday, the Committee on an Appeal for Human Rights held a highly emotional special meeting during which Lonnie King and Herschelle Sullivan resigned but were re-elected. To many people, the agreement seemed to be almost a complete surrender. The students had been presented with almost the same proposals during the summer of 1960 and had rejected them flatly. The objections were so loud and bitter that the leaders of the Student-Adult Liaison Committee decided to call a special mass meeting at which the terms of the agreement would be more fully explained and defended.

The meeting took place on March 10 at the Warren Methodist Church not far from the campus of Atlanta University The church was filled to capacity, and loud speakers were set up outside so that others could listen to the proceedings. Over 2,000 people attended the meeting. The signers of the agreement began by defending its main provisions and by revealing, as evidence of the good faith of the white merchants, that the first of a series of planning sessions for the actual desegregation of the lunch counters had taken place only the preceding afternoon. The audience began growing restless and began heckling the speakers. A. T. Walden pleaded with them to accept the compromise agreement:

Compromise is a part of life, none of us gets all that we want from life . . .
It takes time to get a compromise, but you can't have real social progress
without it . . . What difference does a few months make in social progress?
We've been fighting for this thing for one hundred years; now we have it
within our grasp. Let's have the good sense not to throw it away.

Soon after Walden finished speaking, however, the audience began shouting
down the speakers who were defending the agreement and the chairman lost
control of the meeting. During the confusion a minister, The Reverend
Harold Wilburn, made his way to the platform and began delivering a bitter
denunciation of the agreement. He called for a continuation of the boycott
and shouted: "We don't have to please the downtown merchants; when we
go downtown we aren't begging, we're buying! No self-respecting Negro can
go back downtown under these conditions." This statement received
tremendous cheers of approval, and he concluded by saying: "The downtown
merchants want time, they want to wait to give us what we are entitled to.
Well, let them wait as long as they will, but let us tell them that when they
desegregate, we'll be back downtown!"

In the uproar that followed this speech, calls came from the audience for
a repudiation of those who were responsible for the agreement. Benjamin
Brown, a student leader, tried unsuccessfully to bring the crowd under
control and pleaded for unity and trust in the established leaders. "This is a
crucial time," He shouted, "this is no time to change leadership!" But his
plea was met with demands that new leaders take up the fight, and the
audience was in a turmoil

At this point, Martin Luther King, Jr., dramatically stepped to the
platform to make a statement. As soon as he was introduced, the shouting
ceased and the church grew quiet, a testimony to his enormous prestige.
King spoke solemnly and in measured tones. He deplored the bitter attacks
being made on the leadership and called for a new spirit of trust and
confidence, he called this spirit only an extension of the principles of
nonviolent resistance which had proved so successful in their struggles against
segregation. He praised the agreement, pointing out that it was the first
crack in the resistance to lunch counter desegregation in the Deep South. He
concluded with a plea that the agreement be accepted and that everyone
now turn his attention away from the past and toward the many struggles
yet to come:

We must move out now on the road of calm reasonableness. We must come to a mood of mutual trust and mutual confidence. No greater danger exists for the Negro community than to be afflicted with the cancerous disease of disunity. Disagreements and differences there will be, but unity there must be!

When King sat down the mood of the crowd had been transformed, and the opposition to the agreement was silenced. After the singing of a spiritual the crowd dispersed, and the agreement was saved.

Many Negroes privately continued their boycott of the downtown area, but no more organized protest demonstrations took place. The formal desegregation of the restaurants, lunch counters and restrooms in all major department and variety stores took place, without incident, six months later, on September 27, 1961.

Conclusion: The Struggle Continues

The desegregation of lunch counters in the city's major department stores was a significant step forward for Atlanta's Negro community in its struggle against racial discrimination. It was not the first such victory by any means; the white primary had ended in 1946; Negro policemen had been hired (for duty in the Negro areas only and without full power to arrest white men) in 1948; the city's golf courses and public libraries had also been peacefully desegregated prior to the dispute But the sit-ins had been different. Besides the immediate results provided for by the agreement, these demonstrations of protest had awakened the white community to an awareness of widespread discontent among the Negroes of Atlanta. No longer could they believe those who argued, to quote the student's Appeal, "that everything is fine and equal, and the Negro is happy and satisfied." It was clear now that segregated lunch counters were only one part of a larger pattern of discrimination which the Negroes were determined to destroy,

Also during the dispute over the sit-ms, young, militant Negro leaders took a prominent part in a major community conflict for the first time, and clashed publicly with the established Negro leadership. White civic leaders were especially surprised by this development. They had been accustomed to dealing with a small number of prominent Negroes whose power and influence they had never questioned. Outside of this small circle of exceptional individuals, they knew little about life in the Negro community. To some extent, all Negroes looked alike to them.

These major new developments caused experienced civic and political leaders to make serious miscalculations several times during the controversy over the sit-ins. For example, the management of Rich's, Inc., underestimated the influence and determination of the new, militant leaders when they tried to settle the dispute in the traditional manner by negotiating secretly with only the established Negro leadership. Similar instances of faulty judgment also occurred within the Negro community. Neither the conservative nor the liberal leaders anticipated the angry reaction against them that came as an immediate result of the agreement to end the sit-ins, After the dispute, Warren Cochrane, the secretary of the Atlanta Negro Voters League and a highly regarded Negro leader with long experience in the city, admitted that he had not anticipated the extent to which lower class Negroes would be willing to sacrifice to ensure the success of the student demonstrations. He was surprised at the almost total effectiveness of the boycott in the downtown area, and even more surprised when Negroes who lost their lobs in restaurants and lunch counters which closed because of the demonstrations accepted the hardship and still expressed support for the student movement.

Such frequent misinterpretations of personal attitudes and public moods are an indication of the extent and the rapidity of the changes taking place in Atlanta's political system. Significant new developments were occurring within the Negro community which were rendering obsolete many traditional decision-making procedures and conventional judgments about the political behavior of Atlanta's Negroes. The student demonstrations themselves were indications that significant shifts in attitudes and expectations were occurring. With their demonstrations the students forced adult leaders to express opinions on the propriety of protest, of "direct action" as a tactic to be used in the struggle against segregation. It was this pressure to take sides that aggravated differences among adult Negro leaders which had been slowly developing during the years since World War II.

Confusion and dissension among the leaders of the Negro community resulted in the creation of several new community organizations during the sit-in dispute. The established organizations, such as the NAACP, the Urban League, the Atlanta Negro Voters League, and other professional and fraternal groups were either controlled by conservatives who disapproved of the demonstrations, or were caught in a web of cross-pressures which immobilized the leadership. Organized protest required new organizational weapons, and the Atlanta Committee for Cooperative Action, the Committee on an Appeal for Human Rights, and the Student-Adult Liaison Committee were all created in response to this new set of circumstances.

The most profound impact of the sit-in demonstrations, however, was an intangible, widespread shift in the mood of the Negro community in Atlanta. Numerous observers of the city's political life, both white and Negro, said that there was a perceptible rise in the level of aspirations among the city's Negro citizens in the wake of the demonstrations. For the first time there seemed to be grounds for real hope that racial discrimination might come to an end. Many who for years had been apathetic to politics and efforts to fight segregation seemed to be shaking off the mood of cynical resignation that had paralyzed them in the past. As Martin Luther King, Sr., father of the famous civil rights leader, put it:

> Something wonderful is happening in this town. The low-down Negroes are getting tired. I mean the kind of folks who just come and go like the rain. White folks have never paid them any mind, but they're tired. They just aren't going to take it like they always have before. They're just getting tired.

With this major unsettling force developing in the Negro community it seems unlikely that the Negro drive to break down racial barriers will not stall once a few victories are won. Because of increasing demands for equality from the Negro community and with the explosive issues of housing segregation, discrimination in employment and large scale integration of the public schools still ahead, Negro leaders are likely to become even more aggressive and militant. The indications are that the issue of racial discrimination will dominate Atlanta's politics for some time to come.

The city faces a challenge of long duration. As the younger Negroes begin to look outside the boundaries of the Negro ghetto and yearn for integration into the dominant community, they are not likely to become satisfied until their status or social ranking is arrived at rationally—until they are judged on the basis of their personal attainments, not merely by the color of their skin.

92

Notes

1. This phase comes originally from Floyd Hunter's book, *Community Power Structure*, which was a study of Atlanta. The book has caused considerable uproar in academic circles, and it is, in my view, a much over-simplified treatment of Atlanta's political system. But the fact remains that the phrase is widely used by Negro and white civil rights leaders and journalists all over the South. In this particular case, Lonnie King was referring to the phalanx of leaders, both white and Negro, who controlled the city's large businesses, and its political institutions. King himself felt that the business leaders were the dominant figures, as did most of the Negro leaders I interviewed. Many of them felt that the city's financial elite could get about anything it wanted, so they tried to devise policies to influence it. They put little faith in politicians or political solutions. Of course, this attitude contributed to Mayor Hartsfield's difficulties in solving the sit-in dispute, and thus contributes something of a self-fulfilling prophecy. Almost all of my Negro respondents had heard of Hunter's book and had a vague idea of its thesis, though few had actually read it. Most of them displayed an almost uncritical acceptance of the notion that a small clique of financiers and businessmen actually ran the city from "behind the scenes." It seems likely, therefore, that Hunter's ideas, produced by a professional sociologist and claiming the authority of objective, scientific fact, have done a great deal to enhance the prestige and influence of the city's leading businessmen. By assenting that a hierarchy of influence exists in Atlanta, Hunter may have helped to create, or at least to reinforce, just such a hierarchy.

2. What happened to the white clerks is not known certainly, but it is assumed that they were transferred to other stores in the area. Colonial has at least twenty-five or thirty stores in Atlanta as well as its main warehouse and headquarters. There is also a fairly rapid rate of turnover among employees of grocery stores and the necessary openings might easily have developed during the month of the boycott.

3. This agreement was honored, but Martin Luther King was immediately arrested by a suburban city and changed with breaking his parole from a minor traffic violation. This incident led to the famous phone call to the King family by John F. Kennedy during the 1960 campaign.

The Strategy
of a Sit-In

C. ERIC LINCOLN

ATLANTA

If no wool-hat politicians from the rural counties are loitering about with their ears cocked for subversive conversation, both Negro and white natives are apt to boast that Atlanta is "the New York of the South."

One morning last March, sophisticated Atlanta was rudely jarred by the realization that it was like New York in ways it had never particularly noticed before: its Negro minority was not at all timid about expressing its dissatisfaction and demanding action in no uncertain terms. In fact, there in the morning *Atlanta Constitution* was a full-page advertisement entitled "An Appeal for Human Rights," and the list of rights the Negroes said they wanted ranged all the way from the right of attending the public schools of Georgia on a nonsegregated basis to being admitted to hospitals, concerts, and restaurants on the same basis as anybody else. The home-bound commuters got the same message in a full-page advertisement in the evening *Journal*, which, according to its masthead, "Covers Dixie Like the Dew."

The advertisement, signed by six Negro students representing the six Negro colleges in Atlanta, said in part:

"We, the students of the six affiliated institutions forming the Atlanta University Center—Clark, Morehouse, Morris Brown and Spelman colleges, Atlanta University and the Interdenominational Theological Center—have joined our hearts, minds and bodies in the cause of gaining those rights which are inherently ours as members of the human race and as citizens of the United States . . .

"We do not intend to wait placidly for those rights which are already legally and morally ours . . . Today's youth will not sit by submissively, while being denied all rights, privileges, and joys of life . . .

"We must say in all candor that we plan to use every legal and non-violent means at our disposal to secure full citizenship rights as members of this great Democracy . . . "

The reaction in Atlanta, a city known for its more or less amicable race relations, was swift and vigorous. In the white community there was genuine amazement over the dissatisfaction of the Negro students. After all, in Atlanta many Negroes own expensive homes, run substantial businesses, and practice the professions with a high degree of respect in the community at large.

Predictably, white reaction polarized along urban-rural political lines. Mayor William B. Hartsfield, whose qualifications as a hardheaded Southern liberal are rated high by many of the most militant advocates of Negro rights, praised the statement and said that it "performs the constructive service of letting the white community know what others are thinking."

But a few blocks away in the state capitol, Governor Ernest Vandiver denounced the student appeal as a "left-wing statement . . . calculated to breed dissatisfaction, discontent, discord and evil." The Georgia governor had been elected on a platform of total segregation by a predominantly rural electorate voting under Georgia's so-called county-unit system. Under the county-unit rules, a vote cast by a semi-literate sharecropper in rural Echols County (with a population of 2,494) has ninety-odd times the value of a vote case by an Emory University professor voting in Atlanta, which has a metropolitan population of more than one million. The governor did go so far as to admit that the appeal for human rights was "skillfully prepared"—so well prepared in fact, that "Obviously, it was not written by students." According to Governor Vandiver, "It did not sound like it was prepared in *any* Georgia school or college." (The italics are mine but the grammar is his.)

The governor could have been more generous in his estimate of the quality of education in Georgia. As far as Negroes are concerned, Atlanta, with six private and church-related institutions of higher learning, has long been a unique educational center. It is estimated that at least ten per cent of all Negro Ph.D.s in America received their undergraduate training in Atlanta. And the students of the Atlanta University Center were soon to exhibit a remarkable degree of skill at dramatizing their determination to have the rights to which they feel entitled.

First Skirmishes

The sit-in movement in Atlanta was born in a corner drugstore opposite the Atlanta University Center, when a handful of students from the several Negro colleges found themselves discussing the sit-ins already in progress in North Carolina and elsewhere. A mass meeting at Atlanta University early last March resulted in the formation of a Committee on Appeal for Human Rights, which several days later drew up the statement enumerating their grievances and calling upon "all people in authority . . . all leaders in civic life . . . and all people of goodwill to assert themselves and abolish these injustices."

To test the receptiveness of white Atlantans to the attempted desegregation of public and semi-public facilities, the students sought to attend a musical at the city auditorium with tickets for orchestra seats ordered in advance; and they "sat in" for service at a lunch counter at Rich's, the largest department store in the Southeast. At the municipal auditorium they were permitted to occupy the seats for which they held tickets, but the section in which they sat was promptly designated a Negro section by the management, and seating continued on a *de facto* basis. At Rich's the students were served on March 3 and 4, but thereafter, and without prior notice, they were refused. The Appeal for Human Rights followed, but neither the newspaper advertisements nor attempts at negotiation with Rich's and the other major downtown stores produced results.

At Rich's—which stretches almost a full block on either side of Forsyth Street—one can buy anything from a packet of pins to a passage to Paris. It is generally assumed that from seventy to ninety per cent of the Negroes in Atlanta's business and professional class have maintained accounts there. When no satisfactory agreement could be reached with the management of the store, the students threw picket lines in front of it and urged all Negroes to cancel their accounts and practice "selective purchasing"—that is, to spend their money somewhere else. This was to be the first in a series of skirmishes with the giant store, a kind of field maneuver in preparation for an all-out campaign in the fall.

By the time the colleges were closed for summer vacation, the student movement had taken on some of the aspects of a permanent organization. The Committee on Appeal for Human Rights had developed into a kind of general staff, and several operating committees with specific functions had been set up under its aegis. A Student-Adult Liaison Committee had been established to interpret the student movement to the Negro community and to enlist its support. On this committee were business executives, college presidents, professors, lawyers, other Negro leaders, and students.

The adult members of the liaison committee also served in an advisory capacity on request, but they were excluded from all student meetings dealing with policy and strategy. As one student leader has explained, "We preferred not to embarrass or otherwise discompose our adult leaders: they may have vested interests or personal obligations which may make it difficult for them to share directly in our deliberations, or in our strategy and the implementation of policy." Nonetheless, the sit-ins got overwhelming support from Negro adults, both direct and indirect. For one thing, during the summer a great many adults learned to get along without the convenience of charge accounts at the downtown stores. One group of businessmen underwrote a modest newspaper called the Atlanta *Inquirer*, edited by a college professor and largely staffed by students.

After most of the college students had scattered for their summer vacations, a switch in tactics directed the summer "field maneuvers" at chain grocery stores that have outlets in Negro neighborhoods but discriminate against Negroes in their employment practices. Except for "selective purchasing," the main campaign against the downtown stores was postponed until fall.

The summer "maneuvers" were directed mainly at units of Colonial Stores and at some smaller businesses located in areas with from ninety-five to one hundred per cent Negro patronage. When the stores refused to negotiate with the students on the question of hiring Negroes above the level of menials, picket lines were organized and a selective purchasing campaign was urged upon Negro housewives. The chief target, a Colonial store near the heart of the Negro business district on the city's Northwest Side, suddenly "closed for remodeling." A few days later it reopened with Negroes upgraded in three departments. Shortly thereafter a second store in the Colonial chain hired a Negro cashier and a Negro butcher. Two smaller stores had either already employed Negro salespersons or did so immediately after Colonial changed its policies.

Logistics and Deployment

What came to be referred to as the "Fall Campaign" got under way immediately after the reopening of the colleges in mid-September. This time the main sit-in targets were in the heart of the Atlanta shopping district. Because of its size and its alleged "leadership" in the maintenance of segregated facilities, Rich's became once again the prime objective. Encouraged, however, by the fact that in the seven months since the sit-ins had begun in Greensboro, North Carolina, 112 Southern cities had desegregated lunch counters, the students added Davison-Paxon, the second largest store in Atlanta, as well as drug chains such as Lane-Rexall and Walgreen and the dime and variety stores, including Woolworth, Kress, W. T. Grant, McCrory, Newberry, and H. L. Green. Accommodations were requested at *all* facilities—lunch counters, rest rooms, and in the case of the department stores, restaurants and dining rooms.

The stores refused to negotiate with the students, and beginning on October 19 a succession of sit-ins harassed the downtown merchants and brought out scores of extra police and plainclothes detectives. By Friday, October 21, hundreds of students had launched attacks in coordinated waves. Service to *anyone* at eating facilities in the stores involved had all but ended, and sixty-one students, one white heckler, and Dr. Martin Luther King were all in jail. Under a truce called by Mayor Hartsfield everyone was out of jail by Sunday morning except Dr. King. Negotiations between the merchants and the Student-Adult Liaison Committee were promised on the initiative of the mayor. When the truce ended thirty days later, no progress had been made in settling the impasse, and on November 25, the all-out attack was resumed. By mid-December, Christmas buying was down sixteen per cent—almost $10 million below normal.

Both the Atlanta police and the merchants have been baffled by the students' apparent ability to appear out of nowhere armed with picket signs, and by the high degree of co-ordination with which simultaneous attacks were mounted against several stores at once. Even members of the Ku Klux Klan, dressed in full regalia and prepared to counterdemonstrate against the students, frequently found themselves wandering around the downtown streets bemused—always a jump or two behind the sit-in students. The secret of their easy mobility lay in the organization the students had perfected in anticipation of an extended siege.

Much of the credit for the development of the organizational scheme belongs to Lonnie King, a Morehouse student who is the recognized leader of the student movement in Atlanta, and his immediate "general staff." Policymaking is done by a board of about fifteen students, constituting the Committee on Appeal for Human Rights, which interprets and tries to make effective the wishes of the students of the six colleges who are loosely joined together in what is known as the Atlanta Student Movement. The committee is co-chaired by Lonnie King and Herschelle Sullivan, a twenty-two-year-old senior at Spelman College. Its executive officer has the rather whimsical title of *"le Commandante."*

Le Commandante is Fred C. Bennette, a pre-theology student at Morris Brown College. The headquarters of the movement are in the basement of a church near the University Center, and Bennette arrives there promptly at seven o'clock each morning and goes through a stack of neatly typed reports covering the previous day's operations. On the basis of these reports, the strategy for the day is planned.

By eight o'clock the first contingent of volunteers for the day's assignments has arrived: there may be anywhere between twenty-five and a hundred students present. There is a brief devotional period, which usually concludes with a prayer that the white people of Georgia and throughout the United States will learn to overcome their prejudices, and that the students will be restrained, non-violent, and loving in their attempts to establish human dignity in Georgia. After the devotions, the student volunteers may go to the church kitchen for coffee and doughnuts provided by various adult organizations. They are then likely to scatter about the church looking for places to study until they are summoned for duty.

Meanwhile, *le Commandante* and his staff are in conference. Robert ("Tex") Felder, Deputy Chief of Operations and a second-year student at the Interdenominational Theological Center, will have arrived, as will a fellow student, the Reverend Otis Moss, who serves as field commander for the committee. Morris J. Dillard of Morehouse and James Felder of Clark College, who serve as co-chairmen of a subcommittee on public relations, will be on hand, and *le Commandante* will also expect to hear a report from a Clark College senior, Benjamin Brown, who keeps the organization's books and acts as its treasurer. Telephoned reports from Senior Intelligence Officer Daniel Mitchell, a Clark junior (already at his post downtown), will describe the nature of the flow of traffic at each potential target.

'All Right, Let's Go'

The general staff having concluded its deliberations, a number of pickets selected on the basis of their class schedules and the nature of the day's objectives will be assembled and briefed by Deputy Commander Robert Felder. A large map dividing the downtown district into five areas is invariably consulted and an Area Commander is appointed for each operational district. Assignments fall into three categories: pickets (called by the students "picketeers"), sit-ins, and a sort of flying squad called "sit-and-runs." The objective of the sit-and-runs is simply to close lunch counters by putting in an appearance and requesting service. When the merchants discontinue service to all rather than serve the Negroes, the sit-and-runs move on to another target. The group designated "sit-ins" are prepared to contest their right to be served and are willing to go to jail if need be. Those volunteering for sit-in duty are not to request bail if they are arrested.

By now it is nine or nine-thirty, and transportation has arrived. Cars provided without charge by funeral homes or other businesses as well as by individual housewives and some students are waiting to be loaded. The Deputy Commander provides each driver with a driver's orientation sheet outlining in detail the route to be followed by each driver, and the places where each of the respective groups of students are to be let out. The Area Commanders are given final instructions concerning the synchronization of the attack, and the cars move off, following different routes into the city.

In one of the last cars to leave headquarters will be the Deputy Field Commander, who with a selected squad of "stand-bys" will be driven to his "field headquarters" on the "Ramparts," a designation referring to the steps of the Post Office annex across the street from Rich's department store.

Meanwhile, Field Commander Otis Moss is checking a communications code with Ernest Brown, an eighteen-year-old Morehouse junior, or one of the five other licensed radio operators who man a short-wave radio set up in the church nursery. When this has been attended to, Commander Moss climbs into an ancient automobile equipped with a short-wave sending and receiving unit and heads for the downtown shopping district. He is accompanied by Robert Allen, eighteen, a Morehouse junior majoring in physics, whose job it will be to man the mobile radio unit.

The students have scarcely been deployed before a delivery truck arrives with a crate of apples and a dozen loaves of bread. These are from a small storekeeper who wants to contribute to the cause. Other gifts of food, cigarettes, and soft drinks arrive during the course of the morning. A housewife brings in a half-dozen pies; an insurance executive calls to say that he will underwrite the cost of $115 worth of printing the students have contracted for. A small service station will give a hundred gallons of gasoline. All such gifts are recorded and notes of thanks are written to the donors by members of a subcommittee on community support. By eleven o'clock a group of churchwomen have arrived to prepare lunch for the students.

Reports from the Field and Area Commanders begin to trickle in by radio and telephone. As the lunch hour nears, the volume of reports will increase to one every two or three minutes. The reports are typed and dated and placed on the desk of *le Commandante* by a corps of young women who serve as "Communications Aides." Duplicates are posted on the bulletin board and the students remaining at headquarters crowd around to watch the fortunes of their colleagues downtown. Here are two actual reports taken from the files and approved for publication by the Security Officer:

> 11/26/60   11:05 AM
> *From:* Captain Lenora Tait
> *To: le Commandante*
> Lunch counters at Rich's closed. Proceeded to alternative objective. Counters at Woolworth's also closed. Back to Rich's for picket duty. Ku Klux Klan circling Rich's in night gowns and dunce caps. "Looking good!"

> *From:* Gwendolyn Lee
> *To: le Commandante*
> Sign has been torn from the back of one of our white picketeers. He got another sign and returned to the line. Morale of white picketeers very good. Known heckler, and old man in a gray suit, is on the scene. White opposition increasing. Plainclothes detective made co-ordinator keep moving. All picketeers now in front of Rich's.

The white pickets referred to were from Emory University, a segregated Methodist college in Atlanta. White students from the University of Georgia have also joined the Negro students in the picket lines.

Negro students have sometimes been kicked and beaten, and one student, Elroy Emory of Morris Brown College, has been repeatedly singled out for attack by a group of black-jacketed young white men who come regularly to heckle the Negro pickets. The Ku Klux Klan has mounted counterdemonstrations on at least two occasions, and has threatened to call a white boycott against any store that desegregates its eating facilities.

The downtown merchants and the Atlanta police have deplored the Klan's meddling, as have the Atlanta newspapers. It has been the Negro students who have insisted that the Klan's right to demonstrate ought to be protected. When the Klan turned out in force on Saturday, December 10—red, white, and green satin gowns, hoods and all—to demonstrate against the students and the newspapers, the students called a mass meeting for six o'clock the next morning "to pray for our white brothers of the Ku Klux Klan." Nearly five thousand students and adults made their way to Herndon Stadium before daylight, and stood bareheaded in a cold rain to be led in prayer by the Reverend William Holmes Borders for the spiritual enlightenment of the Ku Klux Klan. That night a bomb wrecked a Negro elementary school a few blocks from the scene of the early-morning prayer meeting.

Allies and Morale

The sit-ins continue, a somber prelude to the school desegregation problems Atlanta will have to face next September. Support from adult Negroes is firm and consistent, and professional men and women have joined the students in the picket lines on "Doctors' Day," "Nurses' Day," and even "Professors' Day."

In some cases the students have been encouraged by white clerks and other personnel working in the very stores against which the sit-ins are directed. At least one sympathetic white woman living in Atlanta's exclusive Buckhead section fired her maid when the maid admitted that she had crossed the picket line at Rich's to buy a dress. Another white woman who had been watching the New Orleans spectacle on television called an official at one of the Negro colleges to ask that the Negroes continue to pray that the white race be forgiven for its behavior toward Negroes and that the students be encouraged to continue their efforts.

There seems little doubt that the efforts will be continued. The Negro students and their white and black allies are determined to keep on sitting in, sitting and running, and picketing until their battle is won.

A Stormy Rally
in Atlanta

LIONEL NEWSOM & WILLIAM GORDEN

The Atlanta, Georgia, Chamber of Commerce and a Liaison Committee representing the Negro community, on March 6, 1961, signed a contract to desegregate city lunch counters. Over seventy eating places were involved and the merchants who signed included most of the prominent downtown department store managers. The national wire services proclaimed a major victory for Atlanta Negroes and praised the Chamber of Commerce for making their city the first in the "hard core" South to negotiate such a broad agreement for orderly desegregation.

But the contract had not been won easily. The settlement was the culmination of a year-long campaign for "human dignity" skillfully conducted by a student committee from the Atlanta University Center, and backed by the majority of the 4,000 Negro students enrolled. The campaign was launched with a full-page advertisement entitled "An Appeal for Human Rights" which appeared in the March 9, 1960, *Atlanta Journal and Constitution*. This candid indictment of Atlanta segregation, labeled left-wing by Governor Ernest Vandiver, concluded with a pledge by the students "to use every legal and non-violent means . . . to secure full citizenship . . ."

And they did. "Kneel-ins," boycotts of supermarkets, mass meetings numbering up to 8,000 Negroes, marches and picketing, and concentrated "sit-ins" provoked many arrests and on-again, off-again negotiations. Meanwhile, within the Negro ranks apathy and conservatism hindered the campaign. The established Negro newspaper, *The Atlanta Daily World*, editorially opposed any direct action and refused student ads advocating boycotting. A new Negro newspaper, sympathetic to the crusade "not to buy segregation," was organized. From the pulpit and college classroom to the picket line outside the department store, pressure in the Negro community united the cold war against the downtown area. In spite of some 500 to 600 Negroes losing their jobs as a result of the lunch counters' closing, the boycott became nearly unanimous for the Negro population (32% of Atlanta). In February 1961, the students, 1,600 strong, picketed the downtown area and a new wave of sit-ins resulted in eighty arrests. Soon after this concentrated effort, the desegregation contract was signed.

Crusade, Contract, Confusion

The week following the historic agreement found the Negro community confused about the terms of the contract. The Chamber of Commerce press release implied an uncertainty: "The Chamber of Commerce . . . announced: 'that the lunchrooms will be reopened on a segregated basis pending a final decision in the Atlanta school issues and that the desegregation will then follow the pattern of that decision.'" Was this another of the white man's delaying tactics? Rumors circulated about the "compromising leadership." The Black Muslims, a small vociferous element advocating black supremacy, published handbills condemning the Liaison Committee for "selling out to the Chamber of Commerce." Many felt uninformed, uncertain, critical, and left out. A student committee of 150 felt that a contract which represented only partial fulfillment of their goals compromised too much and prepared a statement asserting that the contract was a mistake.

The Rally

A special mass meeting was called for March 10, 1961, by the Liaison Committee to clarify and to gain the support of the Negro community for the signed agreement. Over 2,000 persons jammed the Warren Street Methodist Church near the Atlanta University Center. People crowded the doorways and stood outside listening to the meeting from a loud-speaker system. Approximately one-third of the audience was students. All fifteen members of the Student-Adult Liaison Committee were on the platform facing their dark-skinned brethren.

The meeting opened with choruses worded in the new tenacious language of the movement: "Everybody say freedom"; "Don't let nobody turn you 'round"; and "We shall overcome." The "jail-birds," those students who had been arrested for sitting-in, were introduced as heroes who had written many of the stanzas while behind bars.

Following the singing, the Atlanta president of the National Association for the Advancement of Colored People read an explanation of the agreement. His statement denounced the uncertainty of the newspaper releases: ". . . It is not true that the integration of the lunchrooms and other facilities is left to some uncertain 'if or when' situation; nor is it true that it is dependent upon the settlement of the public school issue."

Attorney A. T. Walden, Negro counsel who negotiated the settlement, next interpreted the contract. His brief and oratorical remarks began with praise for the students and "a great town where demonstrations have been possible under law." He assured the audience that the contract was a sound one and that their goal of integrated lunch counters would be attained. "There's no doubt about if it's going to take place; we have it in black and white." No pun was intended. Laughter resulted when he added, "You'll have to take my word for it."

A favorite son among the students, Benjamin Brown, in a two-minute speech, pleasantly but firmly presented the student viewpoint regarding the agreement:

> I come as an individual tonight, but I come representing a viewpoint which I think you ought to know about and this viewpoint is the thinking of the majority of the students which make up Atlanta University Center.
>
> We have great confidence in our leaders, Lonnie and Herschelle, and the persons who signed the agreement. We don't feel they have sold us down the river. (Applause) However, I must make this clear, it is the thinking of the majority of the students that we must continue to stay out from downtown. (Tremendous applause)
>
> I hope by saying this we are not encouraging anyone to go against the agreement. They said we could call off the boycott whenever . . . feasible. Well, we don't feel that this feasible time will come until those counters are desegregated. (Standing ovation)

The signers of the contract had agreed to call off the boycott and sit-ins and picketing "as soon as feasible." Evidently, the students were determined to continue the boycott, and it was not yet clear whether they would discontinue the sit-ins so that the lunch counters could be re-opened. Would the contract be broken?

Another member of the committee, the Reverend Martin Luther King, Sr., was called upon to explain his position. The applause began heartily before "Senior" was announced. When the crowed realized that King, Senior, had been introduced, the applause changed to moderate intensity. King, Senior's, "stand pat" statement was slow and deliberate: ". . . By your saying I've sold out bothers me very little. I keep my record up and my business is to keep any of that from being true . . . If you want the little place I have you can have it. I'm tired, as tired as I can be . . . Now God bless you, and let's keep working together for the good of all of us."

The elder King was typical of many older Negro ministers who had preached moderate integration for years and now had joined the more aggressive student inspired movement. He and the committee were on the right side, but not playing stubbornly enough for the crowd. During the months of sitting-in and boycotting compromise had become a "dirty word."

During the question period which followed, the crowd became difficult to control. Even the pro-sit-in Negro newspaper made this assessment: "The committee found it all but impossible to attempt explanation of the agreement Friday night to an often openly hostile and disrespectful crowd which jammed the aisles . . ."

The hostility reached its climax during the question period which followed the elder King's speech. In the beginning of the question period one of the ministers wanted to make a speech. The chair ruled speeches out of order, but the crowd chanted, "We want Wilburn," until they got Wilburn. The Reverend Wilburn's remarks were inflammatory: "I think the committee ought to realize they represent us. (Applause) I don't think the committee needs to defend itself, but simply ought to come back to report to us. And let us decide whether we think what they've done is adequate or not. (Applause) . . . I simply want to ask you if you thought those students were playing when they went to jail. (Applause and cheers) And when we talk about going downtown to desegregate lunch counters we're not begging, we're buying! (Cheers) . . . It may not be an *if*, but it certainly is a *when* situation. (Long cheers) Now it simply boils down to this, I don't see how in the name of heaven after going through all of this toil, all this suffering and sacrifice, humiliation, downgrading and degrading . . . any self-respecting Negro can go downtown." (Prolonged, standing ovation)

The crowd seemed to enjoy the confusion and this opportunity to exhibit their zealousness as "activists." Here was a chance to release the frustrations and repressions propagated by years of living in a segregated, structured society.

The crowd at another point during the question period impatiently laughed and booed when a committee member talked over his allotted time. The committee member attempted, unsuccessfully nine times, to continue his speech with the phrase "in addition to that." Later one person who got the floor began a personal tirade against the committee: "We are not satisfied with the negotiations . . . I personally denounce the leadership." The crowd booed him down, and at this point Ben Brown coolly called for temperate expression and asserted the general intention of the crowd:

> Ladies and gentlemen, please, ladies and gentlemen, we are upset over this but I think we must keep our heads while we discuss this matter. Students, as I stated before, we are not trying to repudiate our leaders and what they have done. (Applause) This is no time to change leaders. (Applause) Now I think it is the general consensus that we are going to continue our boycott, so let's not get so disturbed and make all these flashy talks and get everyone emotionally aroused. We will never get anything accomplished. We will go out of here with misinformation and misinterpretation. I beg of you as a student who has been in this thing from the beginning, please follow the leadership here who is trying to preside and get his message over to you. Thank you. (Applause)

The questioning then followed a more orderly fashion, but built to a climax when one young lady requested each of the members of the committee who signed the contract, to ask the crowd to "Stay out from downtown." In her question she called out the names of the fifteen members, and cheers followed each. The chairman of the committee replied, "Give her a hand, she has plenty of courage. Yes, she has." He continued, "As one person, not as a member of the committee, I want to ask you to stay out from downtown." The applause and shouts were riotous—the crowd had persuaded the chairman to ask them to continue the boycott!

King, Jr., and Unity

In this turbulent atmosphere which had lasted two and three-quarter hours, the chairman called upon Dr. Martin Luther King, Jr. The crowd heartily approved. There was little doubt that King, Jr., who had become the national symbol of love and non-violence in racial matters, was still their own prophet in Atlanta. So the young Negro so discontented with "second-class citizenship" listened and the rest "fell into line." In his 20-minute

109

impromptu sermon which followed, Dr. King, Jr., was calm, deliberate, and forceful. His tone had both warmth and authority. His specific objective seemed to be unity in the Negro community and backing for the leadership. He did not argue with the student determination to continue the boycott, nor did he endorse it. His arrangement of ideas followed a logical pattern: (1) the Negro is discontented, (2) differences must be solved with mutual respect, and (3) our goals of first-class citizenship will be achieved with a non-violent method. His remarks provided a perspective, a language of resolution, and a prediction of victorious leadership.

Dr. King, Jr., established a perspective for his audience of "Freedom Fighters." He skillfully linked self-interest with idealism: ". . . But these students in Atlanta and throughout the South and throughout the nation have revealed to us that they have felt the palpitation of purpose and that they have taken our deep groans and passionate yearnings and filtered them in their own souls and fashioned them into a creative protest which is an epic known all over our nation."

He also presented a historical-geographical perspective with reference to the May 17, 1954, Supreme Court decision. He spoke of the desegregation of schools and lunch counters in states bordering the South, and the tremendous importance for Atlanta "breaking the chain of massive resistance in the hard-core South."

The style of Dr. King's sermon contained a loftiness of language which raised the level of resolution above petty in-fighting. He said the misunderstandings are never solved "trying to live in monologue; you solve it in the realm of dialogue." The non-violent technique is "more than a tactic—it is a way of life." But King's flowery language did not disregard the variation in socio-economic status of his audience. In one breath he would use such phrases as: ". . . The rhythmic beat of the deep rumblings of discontent taking place here tonight is indicative of . . ." and in another: "We must see in this struggle that Aunt Jane, who knows not the difference between 'you duz' and 'you don't,' is just as significant as the Ph.D. in English."

The conflicts within the Negro community were minimized as he pointed to the common enemy, "the giants of vested interest, giants of political dynasties, economic power structure, giants of irrational emotionalism." He appealed to a revolt against "the social structure" bigger than lunch counters. We must not rest until segregation is removed from every area of Atlanta life. Biblical allusions with a modern interpretation permeated the address, such as "Caleb and Joshua have been over. They have come back with a minority report saying that we can possess the land in spite of the giants." Thus, King associated self-interest with the religious motive appeal—theirs was a holy crusade.

During the speech, the younger King did not hesitate to use the authority of his role in influencing the crowd. He had earned his right of leadership, and ethos was obviously wielded. Perhaps his personal prestige could reconcile the rift between the crowd and the leadership: ". . . If I had been on that committee that met Monday afternoon, I wouldn't mind anybody saying, Martin Luther King, Jr., you made a mistake. I wouldn't mind anybody saying, Martin Luther King, Jr., you should have thought it over a little longer. I wouldn't have minded anybody saying to me, Martin Luther King, Jr., maybe we made a tactical blunder. But I would have been terribly hurt if anybody said to me, Martin Luther King, Jr., you sold us out! (Applause) I would have been hurt by that."

The conclusion of the sermon was an extended analogy: "If I can use an analogy, we have brought the football of civil rights to about the fifty-yard line." Developing the analogy, he spoke of a great team of linemen with the proper leaders in the backfield, and he predicted crossing the goal line of human dignity. The delivery of the conclusion increased in rate and intensity, but didn't approach the frenzied antiphonal chant noticeable in some Negro sermons. However, it was stirring, and the crowd seemed to know that the rally was over. The song leader said, "If we made a mistake, it's going to be the most significant mistake in Atlanta. If some of us stumbled, it made the rest of us stand up." He then started the old Negro spiritual, "I Know I Got Religion."

The Reverend Martin Luther King, Jr.'s, sermon was a satisfying climax to the rally. He "filled full" his role as their messiah. Wisely avoiding a power-struggle, King, Jr., has not politically bossed either the national or the local organizations associated with the movement. Rather with prestige quotient high, he waits to be called upon as a resource: a sage of the creative approach and spokesman for the cause. With masterful language he had re-affirmed the non-violent strategy and prophesied victory. Perhaps most of all, Dr. King spoke with completeness to that audience because he honored the voice of the congregation. Though he chided the crowd for "irrational emotionalism" and the leadership for possibly a "tactical blunder," he persuaded both of the importance of better communication, of "dialogue" with the representative, democratic framework of their movement.

Immediately following the rally several of the committee seemed exhausted and sobered by the disrespect of the crowd and stated that this was not a typical rally. In later interviews, the student committee chairman made to these writers three observations about the rally: (1) the settlement had been clarified by firsthand knowledge, (2) the sit-ins and picketing would be discontinued, but the boycott was unofficially continued, and (3) from now on, contracts likely would not be signed without first holding something in the nature of a public hearing in the Negro community.

Orderly Desegregation

In the months following the agreement, Atlanta merchants and the Liaison Committee planned orderly desegregation. Members of the Liaison Committee stated to the authors that they felt sure the merchants were aware the boycott was continuing, but that neither party mentioned this during these desegregation planning sessions. Apparently the merchants were satisfied just to be able to keep their lunch counters open without worrying about sit-ins and picketing. The trials of the students arrested in the last sit-ins, scheduled for April 25, 1961, were postponed indefinitely upon the request of the merchants. Atlanta had a contract to fulfill.

During the summer, the race for mayor of Atlanta developed around the segregation issue. Mr. Ivan Allen, who, as chairman of the Chamber of Commerce, had signed the desegregation agreement, became the favored candidate. The retiring mayor and the *Atlanta Constitution*, the leading newspaper, supported Allen. His chief opposition, Lester Maddox, was chairman of the White Citizens' Council. In the run-off election on September 22, 1961, a record vote of over 100,000 favored Allen nearly two-to-one. This vote of confidence and the quietly enforced desegregation of several Atlanta high schools assured the success of the contract for lunch counter desegregation.

An estimated 250 Negroes, divided into small groups, were served at sixty-five to seventy lunch counters almost simultaneously on September 29, 1961. Thus began a week of orderly controlled desegregation, after which integration followed its natural course with no serious conflicts in the following year. Atlanta had understood the determination of the educated Negro citizen—had honored the most sweeping desegregation agreement in the deep South—and the Atlanta victory echoes in integration rallies in other southern cities.

The Atlanta Sit-In

Movement, 1960-1961:

An Oral Study

VINCENT D. FORT

Dedicated to
my father, mother, and son—
Charles, Clara, and Zan

Contents

Introduction 119

I. "Why the Hell Can't I?" 123

II. "It Was in the Air" 129

III. "The Time for Action is Now" 139

IV. "Something We Feel We Got To Do" 145

V. "I Had To Be With Them" 155

Conclusion: "The Struggle is Still Going On" 167

Notes 169

Bibliography 177

This paper was originally written as a Master's thesis in the Department of History at Atlanta University in 1980. It was been edited for publication, but otherwise is presented here as it was written.

Vincent Fort is a professor of history at Morehouse College. He is presently a Ph.D. Candidate at Emory University and his research interests continue to be the civil rights movement and oral history.

Introduction

This study is an examination of the Atlanta student sit-in movement of 1960-1961 from the inside out. While many articles, dissertations, books essays, and even one novel[1] have been concerned (either wholly or partially) with certain aspects of the Atlanta student movement none of them has provided a view of how the movement was organized, the effects it had on the students, and on their relations with other groups in the Atlanta University Center from where the movement emanated.[2] In doing this it has been necessary to provide a background to explain the influences that made the students eager to protest.

At some points it was necessary to focus on things which occurred outside of the A.U.C. environment, so as to show the relationship between the students and their parents, to give a whole picture of how the sit-ins were organized and, finally, to explain the factors which influenced the students prior to the protests. Still, the emphasis is on what went on in the Center.

To fulfill this emphasis the approach of the study is from an intra-group perspective. The viability of such a direction was reinforced by *Conflict and Competition: Studies in the Recent Black Protest Movement*, a collection of essays which stresses intragroup and interracial conflict in civil rights protests.[3] An even stronger theoretical basis was found in an unpublished paper prepared by the Social Science Division of the Tuskegee Institute in May, 1960, in which the conflict among students, administrators. and faculty as a result of the student movement at Tuskegee was discussed. It provided an intra-institutional framework which sharpened the theoretical base for this study.[4] So, by definition, this thesis is intragroup and intraracial in that the locale it is concerned with is predominantly black. More specifically it is intra-institutional.

Most importantly, this is an oral-based study. Not a great deal of material exists that relates to the events in the A.U.C. during the student movement. More attention was paid to the sit-ins, pickets, marches, kneel-ins, boycotts, and other types of protests that went on in the streets. Less attention was paid to what went on behind closed doors, in classrooms, planning sessions, and discussions on campus among students and their elders. As one scholar

119

of the movement has said, publicity throughout the civil rights movement was more readily given to the march as it came down the street during protests but little to the organizational efforts that went into the march before it turned that corner.[5] Thus, to research the Atlanta student movement it was necessary to go to the students, faculty members, college presidents, and parents who, in their own unique ways, contributed to it.

You have taken up the deep groans of the century. The students have taken the passionate longings of the ages and filtered them in their souls and fashioned a creative protest. It is one of the glowing epics of the time . . .

Martin Luther King, Jr.

to Founder's Day audience at Spelman College on April 10, 1960. *Spelman Messenger*. May 10, 1960, p. 13.

ONE

"Why in the Hell Can't I?"

Before the Atlanta sit-ins began in 1960 several events had occurred to create an atmosphere for making protest a valid option for black students. There were ingredients that combined to form a protest commitment, that is, a dedication and basis for challenging segregation and white supremacy with aggressive nonviolent direct action.

These ingredients varied with each of the student informants giving different observations on the subject. What is unique about the sit-in movement is its spontaneity, but the situation did not exclude certain antecedent factors from playing an important role in making it possible for that spontaneity to come alive.

Julian Bond, a student at Morehouse in 1960, discussed those things he thought to be motivating factors for A.U.C. students. The Montgomery bus boycott (1955-1957) was a prominent factor:

> . . . The Montgomery bus boycott was very much on people's minds. That had been two or three years before. What was significant about the bus boycott, I think, was that for the first time in the civil rights movement which was on everybody's consciousness, but it was a movement of professional people. You had to file a suit. That's what the civil rights movement was about.
>
> So, the ordinary person, a student said, 'Oh, I can't do that. I might give a dollar or something, but I'm not a lawyer. I can't file a suit. I'm not a professional person.'
>
> So, the Montgomery Bus boycott democratized the civil rights movement. It made it possible for anybody to do anything.[1]

Bond went on to say his "real respect and admiration was for the people of Montgomery." The persons he had respect for were the self-sacrificing ones who, despite an aversion to walking, did so during the bus boycott. "Here I am a college student, I'm going to be . . . in the elite. Here's this illiterate, uneducated woman and she's making this sacrifice. Why in the hell can't I?"[2]

123

James Forman, former Student Nonviolent Coordinating Committee chairman, in his autobiographical treatment of the black liberation movement, told of a Spelman student's impressions at the time of the Montgomery bus boycott: "I remember Ruby Doris (Smith) Robinson . . . [a student at Spelman College when the sit-ins began] saying that when she was thirteen or fourteen and saw those old people walking down there in Montgomery, just walking, walking, it had a tremendous impact." Forman commented that the bus boycott "had a particularly important effect on young blacks and helped to generate the student movement of 1960."[3]

A series of events which stood out in Bond's mind just as much as, if not more than, the democratizing effects of the Montgomery Movement was the struggle to integrate public schools during the late fifties and early sixties in such places as Little Rock, Arkansas and New Orleans, Louisiana. These thrusts against segregated schools produced figures for the sit-in college students to emulate: ". . . we saw these younger students doing these things [and] we said, 'hey, we can't let these burdens fall on our younger brothers and sisters. We can do something.'"

He told of something he watched on television:

> I remember watching a girl by the name of Elizabeth Eckford in [Little Rock].
> She came home after a day of school and her mother said her dress was so
> wet with spit she could wring it out. I said, 'my God,' here is a sixteen year
> old girl walking through these vicious, vicious white people and letting them
> spit on her and she's strong enough to take it. Strong enough to take it.[4]

A local newspaper article supports this identification with the struggles of younger students to integrate public schools. A group of students from the A.U.C. was interviewed after the "Appeal for Human Rights" was published on March 9, 1960 but before the first sit-ins of March 15, 1960. The reporter commented that one student believed "total, immediate public school integration is possible." Another student was quoted as saying "I don't feel sorry for the girl who walked through the lines of soldiers and entered Central High School [in Little Rock]. I was proud of her. I'd do it myself, and if I had a daughter I would gladly have her do it."[5]

Farther from home the contact some students had with other countries was a source of discontent among them. Students who had a chance to travel to foreign countries discovered the absence there of the racist segregationist structure they experienced in the United States. When they were accepted on a more just basis abroad, but treated as inferiors in Atlanta, they began to question that structure and were ready to protest.

An example of this readiness can be found among males, in Lonnie King of Morehouse, for whom the armed services functioned as a vehicle from which to see another world, an environment which was not dominated by Jim Crow: ". . . there were a number of students who had been in the Korean conflict who had gotten out of the service in '56 and '57, some even as late as '58, and who had come back to the Center and who had the opportunity to see or experience first hand a more open society that was present in Atlanta, Georgia."[6] King, himself, was stationed in Korea. On his way back to the United States in 1957 he told a friend, "I was coming back to Atlanta when I got out, and this is the corny part. I told him that I believe one thing, that there's going to be a revolution in the South and I want to be there, be a part of it."[7] When the sit-ins began he had the chance to be one of the most important individual parts of the movement.

Another one of these returning veterans spent one and one-half years in Germany. When he came back to Atlanta he became "depressed when he returned home and encountered the strictures of segregation once again." He decided to leave Atlanta as soon as he could earn enough money. Before he could do so the student movement had begun and he became "one of the most active and militant leaders in town."[8]

At Spelman College, a woman's institution, other students were exposed to foreign countries through the Merrill Scholarship Program which allowed recipients to study and travel in Europe.[9] While in Europe the Spelman students got insights into what less race-conscious societies, where racial segregation was absent, were like. Marian Wright, a Spelman student who returned from Europe in August 1959 wrote of the effects of her time abroad: "I have become an individual—aware of personal and national shortcomings and determined to correct these in every instance afforded me. I have felt the sufferings of others and gained incentive to alleviate it in my own way."[10] Wright, Roslyn Pope, and Herschelle Sullivan, all leaders of the student movement at Spelman were recipients of Merrill Scholarships. Sullivan became co-chair of the student protest organization, the Committee on Appeal for Human Rights.[11]

While the Montgomery bus boycott, public school integration, and exposure to foreign countries all played an important part in creating the commitment of students to attempt integration of downtown lunchcounters in Atlanta, no factor was more important than the personal experiences of the students themselves. Personal contacts with segregated lunchcounters, restaurants, restrooms, water fountains, theaters, and buses were constant reminders to Atlanta's black students (and Atlanta's black community, in general) that they were afforded second-class citizenship, at best, in a white racist society. This created emotional responses among which anger and humiliation were prominent. One very involved student activist, Charles Black, affirmed: "We always had the discontents, I suppose, having been reared and having experienced all the routine indignations you know: bus problems, rest-room problems, downtown lunchcounters. It was just, I suppose, a keg of dynamite waiting for a light on the fuse."[12]

Mary Ann Smith Wilson, a student at Morris Brown College, emphasized the effect of day-to-day living under segregation. More than all the other things, the force of being assaulted by the injustice of Jim Crow left an indelible mark on her.

> I can remember some instances of segregation. For the most part I lived in my own world, totally separate from whites and really feeling I had just about everything because I wasn't exposed to what else was out there.
>
> So . . . we had our social activities: the debutante ball, and all those things and I didn't feel deprived at all except for one thing that happened to me when I was in about ninth grade in high school.
>
> I got on the bus and at this time there were mostly students on the bus. The bus was completely filled with [black] students. You'd get on the bus and you'd just sit about anywhere.
>
> I got on the bus and sat on the first seat which was on the side. I happened to look towards my right . . . and there was this white woman sitting next to me. Out of complete shock I just jumped up. I was petrified that I had sat down next to this white lady.
>
> That was the first realization that I had that segregation was having an effect or what it meant to go downtown and not be able to go to a restaurant. And to go downtown and have to go to a separate water fountain. I think something stuck with me about that incident.[13]

That incident began Ms. Wilson's searching herself for the reasons why she had acted as she did. It created a feeling which engendered a receptivity to protest. Ms. Wilson poignantly explained. "We thought why should we go on living like this, why should I raise children and let them be treated like that?" So ". . . when the opportunity came that maybe we can fight this thing, that we don't have to live with it, that there is a way to fight against it . . . we all just rallied toward the focal point of—now we can do something about it."[14]

Carolyn Long, a student at Clark College had experiences similar to that of Ms. Wilson:

> . . . We were always brought up in a very sheltered family. And we never went downtown shopping . . . very infrequently. So, we were not . . . forced to really sit in any particular place.
>
> We always went shopping at a time when we ate before we went . . . [but] it dawned on us, I guess, what we must have been like in seventh, eighth grade that we couldn't try clothes in [the] same places [as whites]. That we couldn't try on clothes at all in some places.
>
> What bugged me more than anything else was the white and black water fountains. I remember just deliberately going to the white fountain to see what would happen. Nothing ever did.[15]

On the way to the Catholic school she was enrolled in, the only white school in Atlanta which would accept black children, it was necessary for Ms. Long to take the bus downtown and then transfer. While the bus she took to downtown had a mostly black ridership, the one she transferred to had a mostly white ridership. Then "we had to go to the back of the bus. Of course I refused to do that . . . It was like I'm a person, you know. I really didn't feel anything [such as inferiority]." She went on: "I saw signs that said 'colored' and 'white' and that bugged me to no end. And I said, 'I'm going to do something about it in my own quiet way,' never imagining as a child that I would be involved in the student movement."[16] Whether she had expected to or not, Ms. Long later became involved with other black Atlanta college students "to do something" about racial injustice in Atlanta.

TWO

"It Was
in the Air"

Isolated incidents of protest without organization would have been easily defeated. It is the objective of this and the next chapter to examine how the students organized their protests; succeeding chapters will discuss how their organizing efforts affected their abilities to take care of academic responsibilities, and their relations with parents, faculty members, and college presidents.

On February 1, 1960 four black freshmen from North Carolina A and T College—Franklin McCain, Ezell Blair, Joseph McNeil, and David Richmond—sat down at a Woolworth lunchcounter in Greensboro. They asked for service, which was promptly denied, with the explanation that blacks were not served at the counter. By the time the four students returned the next day the media had spread news of the "sit-ins" and other black students in the South moved quickly to duplicate the Greensboro protest for the rights of all people to be served at lunchcounters and restaurants regardless of race. Between January, 1960 and August of the next year, 110 cities had desegregated public accommodations as a result of student efforts. Seventy thousand demonstrators participated in various types of protests and some four thousand went to jail.[1]

Atlanta was one of those 110 cities. The meeting that began the organization of the Atlanta sit-in movement is one of the most storied events in the history of the recent civil rights movement.[2] From that initial meeting came what an observer has characterized as "one of the largest and best organized sit-in demonstrations of all."[3]

On February 5, 1960, just four days after the Greensboro sit-ins, Lonnie C. King approached Julian Bond at a student gathering place to solicit his help in organizing sit-in protests in Atlanta.[4] Julian Bond said: "I was first approached by a fellow student at Morehouse when I was sitting [in] what was then Yates and Milton Drugstore at the corner of Chestnut and Fair [streets across from the A.U.C. campus]. This guy [Lonnie King] came up to me and argued with me that he and I, together, should call a meeting to organize sit-in demonstrations in Atlanta."[5] King was carrying a copy of the *Atlanta Daily World*, the city's black-owned newspaper. Pointing to the newspaper's headline which announced new developments in the Greensboro sit-ins King asked Bond, "Don't you think something like that ought to happen here?" and "Don't you think . . . that we ought to make it happen?" While cool to King's urgings at first, Bond soon began actively recruiting students at the drugstore along with King and fellow Morehouse student Joe Pierce.[6]

King was fearful that the opportunity which the events in Greensboro offered would be lost if the initiative was not taken advantage of immediately. He had been in Oklahoma in 1958 when sit-ins had been started there by a NAACP youth chapter. His position "was that the situation in Greensboro would again be another isolated incident in black history, if others didn't join in to make it become something the kids ought to be doing."[7]

Fellow students were asked to meet that day in Sale Hall Annex on the Morehouse campus. In the days following as the sit-in movement grew in intensity throughout the South more and more black Atlanta college students became aware of the rumblings of protest that were occurring in the region. Mary Ann Smith Wilson remembered that "it was in the air certainly" and the initial discussions about the viability of sit-ins began at Morehouse.[8] Alton Hornsby, another Morehouse student, gave an indication of the way in which students were thinking at the time:

> We . . . began talking about them [sit-ins]. The general reaction, as I recall it, was 'this is a move in the right direction.' Then as the days went on there was some talk of 'why aren't we in it?' That seems to have been pretty widespread at the time.[9]

Hornsby's first "awareness" of anything overt being planned was when "they [student leaders] came to the assembly and began outlining the problems and proposals to us. They emphasized pretty much what we knew about the racist segregationist conditions in Atlanta." The student leaders asked for and received voted approval from the student body at Morehouse on "resolutions and demands" to be put to the white establishment. The demands as written suggested "if they were not met we would have to take direct action."[10] After hearing of the North Carolina sit-ins, Carolyn Long remembers the students in Atlanta "wanted ours to be an organized, out-front, combined effort with all the universities involved, the colleges."[11] Julian Bond shared Long's view:

> There were committees and chairmen and [we] tried to have representation from every school. We really always insisted that this not become a Morehouse-Spelman or Morehouse-Spelman-Clark affair.
> Even though Morris Brown was physically separated from the rest of the campus and there wasn't as much back and forth as there is now. And people at Atlanta University were older but we wanted them with us . . . So, we tried deliberately to build that in.[12]

On that first day, February 5, 1960, about twenty students came together at the call of King, Bond, and Pierce. From this group came the student organization, the Committee on Appeal for Human Rights, with Lonnie King as chairman. The most urgent question facing the students was: when would they sit-in? Dr. Benjamin Mays, President of Morehouse College, maintains the first sit-ins were scheduled for February 12 but "postponed because they wished to involve as many Center students as possible." His source for this is Lonnie King.[13]

While the sit-ins were being planned, the students took part in "workshops and seminars on the techniques of nonviolence, picketing and sit-ins."[14] On the subject of nonviolence "there was no dispute in anyone's mind about the use of nonviolence . . ."[15]

In fact, the Committee on Appeal for Human Rights (COAHR) required all of those who demonstrated to take an oath of nonviolence.[16]

If there was no dispute over the use of nonviolence in the Atlanta sit-in movement, there was surely disagreement among the students about who would lead the movement. The dispute appears to have been between a graduate student group at Atlanta University and undergraduates at the other institutions which formed the COAHR. The Atlanta University group was advised by Dr. Lonnie Cross, chairman of the A.U. mathematics department. While one scholar suggested that the A.U. group was the more militant, the chairman of the COAHR maintains "I think the A.U. students really did not want to follow undergraduates.[17] Even though the A.U. faction organized after the COAHR they did hold the first sit-ins, which were, for the most part, ignored and ineffectual.[18] Lonnie King recalled the situation:

> . . . They didn't have the troops. The troops were behind us. And we took the position that when we did it everybody needs to be in it. It shouldn't be A.U.

today and Spelman the next day. 'All of us are niggers' was the expression. So, it didn't make sense for us to go down there and further emphasize the fragmentation in the black community where every [individual] campus was going to go down there . . .

The people at A.U. basically told me to go to hell on that. But the president of A.U., Dr. Clement, supported me. He thought I was right. So, that caused a little conflict.

I remember once we had a big meeting . . . with all the A.U. students wherein Dr. Clement and I spoke and Lonnie Cross and his people spoke. We had a tremendous debate at Bumstead Hall.

I made my position clear to them and Dr. Clement backed me up. Dr. Cross challenged Clement saying that 'we should not stand for another segregated day.'

Nice rhetoric but you're losing sight that if each school had gone down there fighting for the banner then we would have been setting ourselves up for a divide and conquer kind of thing.[19]

There were other, more subtle, disagreements between students. Some students objected to the style of some of the student leadership. Alton Hornsby conceded that, as in any social movement, friction between the assumed leaders and the led emerged: "We had . . . a group . . . of very strong activists who took the position that they had a monopoly on what should be done and how it should be done." Hornsby and "several" others were "offended by that particular approach." Hornsby "agreed with most" but "did not agree with all" of the core leadership's mandates or decisions. Thus, he sat in and demonstrated "when I wanted to sit-in . . . I knew where we were going to be. I'd go down and relieve somebody [or picket and march]."[20]

Lonnie King also realized that tensions might arise. At Morehouse the sit-ins allowed for a "different kind of leadership to emerge." Fraternity members, honor students, and student government association officers were not the sit-in leaders who came out of Morehouse, which produced a conflict recognized by King, who explained: "Some of the [established student] leaders [wondered] why were some of us [Julian Bond, King, etc.] in charge rather than them."[21] At Spelman, Morris Brown, and Clark, by contrast, the "established" student leadership were, for the most part, sit-in leaders.

When the students' plans to take direct action became apparent the A.U.C. presidents became concerned that the students did not take actions which they judged to be dangerous or too radical. They called in the students and advised them to refrain from demonstrations. Subsequently, when the students made it clear that they would take direct action against downtown segregation, the presidents persuaded them to make a unique move before demonstrating, suggesting that the students write "An Appeal for Human Rights" to be published in the Atlanta daily newspapers.[22]

The "Appeal" told of the racist conditions under which black people in Atlanta suffered in the areas of education, voting, medical care, entertainment, recreation, and justice. It closed by saying, "We must say in all candor that we plan to use every legal and non-violent means at our disposal to secure full citizenship rights as members of this great Democracy." Most important among the members of the student committee writing the document, according to Lonnie King and Julian Bond, was Roslyn Pope of Spelman College.[23] Bond, King, Carolyn Long, Herschelle Sullivan (Spelman), and Morris Dillard (Morehouse), also contributed to its composition.[24] Supporting data were based on a pamphlet produced by the Atlanta Council for Cooperative Action, made up of young black businessmen and professionals, titled *Atlanta: A Second Look*.[25]

After the "Appeal" was published the students disavowed publicly rumors that they would, as other southern black students were doing, sit-in and engage in other types of demonstrations. On March 13, 1960 one student told a newspaper reporter: "Don't worry about mass demonstrations. Watch out for something original." Despite this pronouncement students were then preparing themselves for sit-ins by doing such things as counting the number of seats at lunchcounters in downtown businesses for tactical purposes.[26]

Initially, the students planned to sit-in at private lunchcounters, but there was concern that in a court case they would be more likely to lose a dispute over privately owned segregated lunchcounters.[27] Instead, students sat in at downtown lunchcounters directly involved in interstate commerce or leased from the federal government in federal buildings.[28]

When the students approached a lawyer in Atlanta to represent them, they were discouraged by the high fee quoted. Finally, Attorney Donald L. Hollowell acted as counsel for many of the students.[29]

With preparations in progress, it was necessary to select those students who would invade downtown Atlanta to sit-in. Ruby Doris Smith of Spelman College remembered: "I began to think about it [sit-ins] happening in Atlanta, but I wasn't ready to act on my own. When the student committee was formed in the Atlanta University Center, I told my sister [Mary Ann Smith], who was in the student council at Morris Brown College, to put me on the list. And when two hundred students were selected for the first demonstration, I was among them."[30]

The sit-ins began at 11:00 A.M. on March 15, 1960. Seventy-seven students were arrested at City Hall, the State Capitol, Fulton County Courthouse, two office buildings on Peachtree Street where federal employees ate, two railroad stations, and the Trailways and Greyhound bus depots' lunchcounters.[31]

After these initial sit-ins the students wanted to keep the issues of racial discrimination prominent in the public mind. In order to do this the students began picketing chain grocery stores in April to make them increase the number of blacks employed and upgrade the types of jobs they held.[32] While the picketing of the groceries stores proceeded the students wanted to organize a large demonstration to dramatize their objectives. The result of this planning was a march through downtown Atlanta with a stop at the state capitol.

On May 15, at a NAACP-sponsored "state-wide freedom rally" on Morehouse's campus, King announced that the students were going to march on May 17 through downtown to a rally at the Wheat Street Baptist Church on Auburn Avenue to commemorate the sixth anniversary of the Supreme Court decision in the *Brown v. Topeka, Board of Education* case, stopping on the way at the state capitol to further publicize their grievances. Newspaper attention to the announcement made it difficult for King, as chairman of the COAHR and leader of the student movement, to cancel or modify the march after Governor Ernest Vandiver made it clear he would have state troopers waiting to "protect" the state capitol from the students. Dr. Mays and the other A.U.C. presidents tried to persuade King to put the march off, fearing violence on the part of the state troopers, but King decided to go ahead as planned.[33]

The students left the Trevor-Arnett Library on the A.U. campus for the downtown area on their way to the state capitol. As the contingent of 2,000-3,000 students approached the capital, King, at the head of the march, was stopped by the Chief of Police, Herbert Jenkins, who instructed him either to divert the march or be arrested. In King's words:

> What a lot of people haven't understood is that I was out there as the main person on the line. Whereas the college presidents were concerned about that number of students that were at their schools, I had all the students behind this one young guy [himself].
>
> Hell, I wasn't sure I was always right . . . so I said what happens if . . . hundreds of kids get beaten up down here because I'm the man . . . that faced this monster. So, I made the decision to divert the march.

There were some students, between one and four hundred, who lagged behind the main contingent, did not realize the march had been diverted and actually got to the state capitol. These marchers passed the capitol and the troopers unscathed except for jeers and cursing from a mob of whites that had gathered.[34]

After this action the students were faced with the fact that the lunch counters were still segregated and with the possibility that the movement might fall apart as the summer vacation approached and the students dispersed. Mary Ann Smith Wilson told of plans for preventing this: ". . . it was decided we wanted to maintain some kind of intact organization during the summer so we got an office downtown on Auburn [Avenue]."[35] The students spoke to various community and church organizations. A liaison committee was organized to set up such contacts and, according to Lonnie King, ". . . we spent the whole summer doing that [organizing student-community relations]."[36] The presentation made to community groups was called "The Student Movement and You."[37]

During the summer, kneel-ins at white Atlanta churches were organized.[38] Suits also were filed by students in Federal District Court attacking segregated cafeterias at the county courthouse, city hall, and the state capitol.[39]

The students put out a newsletter entitled, as their summer organizing effort was, *The Student Movement and You*.[40] This evolved into the *Atlanta Inquirer* which began publication on July 31, 1961 as a weekly newspaper manned mostly by students in the A.U.C. with the advisement of faculty members, under the editorship of M. Carl Holman, professor of humanities at Clark College. Julian Bond was heavily involved in the newspaper as managing editor, reporter, and columnist and Lonnie King contributed a column entitled "Let Freedom Ring" which was ghostwritten by Bond. The paper was conceived of as an alternative to the black-owned *Atlanta Daily World* which urged a cessation to the sit-ins and other protests in editorials after the initial action in March, 1960.[41]

The boycott which the spring picketing of grocery stores had begun heightened during the summer with Rich's department store, the most prestigious in the city, as its focus. "If we can topple Rich's," was King's theory, "all we have to do is just kind of whisper to the others . . ." In speaking to people in the community he continued, "we showed 'em where it wasn't going to hurt them. We showed them where we were going to the shock troops, we were taking the chances. All we're asking you to do is just stay at home." And it worked. The students impressed upon the community the injustice of segregated eating facilities, water fountains, and restrooms in establishments where they spent money on clothing and other items. The adults were asked to "close out your charge account with segregation, open up your account with freedom."[42]

When school opened in the fall of 1960 the students were anxious to begin their most extensive assault against segregation in downtown Atlanta. Some, as Lonnie King recounts, were too anxious: "A lot of students wanted to go gung-ho in September when we first came back, but we wanted to stage the thing in the middle of October, because we wanted to influence, if we could, the presidential election of 1960, believe it or not." King and Herschelle Sullivan, co-chair of the COAHR, had decided in order to dramatize this thing we ought to get Martin Luther King, Jr. arrested, if we could." Bernard Lee and A. D. King, both students at Morris Brown proposed that they go ahead with demonstrations in September, as opposed to waiting until October, as Lonnie King and Herschelle Sullivan planned to do. King and Sullivan sought to get M. L. King arrested during a demonstration and then send telegrams to presidential candidates John Kennedy and Richard Nixon requesting them to take a position on the movement. The COAHR finally approved the King-Sullivan plan.

Sullivan was delegated the responsibility of calling civil rights movement leader Rev. Martin Luther King, Jr. who had moved back to Atlanta from Montgomery, Alabama, that year. Initially, Dr. King refused Sullivan's request to participate in the Atlanta sit-ins, since he was then on probation for a traffic violation conviction and knew he would be liable to a severe sentence if he were arrested in a sit-in protest. Sullivan located Lonnie King at the Spelman library where he was speaking to other students, and related M. L. King, Jr.'s message. Subsequently, Lonnie King spoke to the minister himself, with the appeal that "you are the spiritual leader of the movement, and you were born in Atlanta, Georgia, and I think it might add tremendous impetus if you would go." The movement leader then agreed to participate and accept arrest.[43]

During September and October before the sit-ins with Rev. King that began the fall campaign, the students made elaborate logistical preparations. Anywhere from twenty-five to one hundred students arrived daily at COAHR headquarters at the Rush Memorial church on Chestnut Street near the A.U.C. campus to help either in the office or in the community to gain support for the movement.[44]

Then, as late October approached, the students were prepared to implement the careful planning that had gone on during the summer. They knew it would not be easy but they also knew the alternative was even less easy to live with.

THREE

"The Time for Action is Now"

The fall sit-ins began on October 19, 1960. As planned, Rev. Martin Luther King, Jr., participated and was arrested along with fifty-one others. All of the arrests were made at the downtown Rich's store, while the other department stores' lunchcounters (Davison's, H.L. Green, Woolworth, Newberry's, Grant's, McCrory's) were closed down. Charges against sixteen of those arrested were dismissed, and the other thirty-six were bound over for trail, including Dr. King. They pleaded innocent and refused to accept bail.[1]

The sit-ins continued and were well coordinated. On October 20, twenty-six more students were arrested. In addition to department and drugstores students sat in at a lunchcounter in the railroad station. Estimates vary from several hundred to two to three thousand as to the number of students who participated.[2] On October 21, only two arrests were made.[3]

The organizing efforts of the students were polished with certain students agreeing to remain seated after they were asked to leave during a sit-in. These students were then arrested and refused bail, as stated, to dramatize the situation. Others moved from lunchcounter to lunchcounter after having been refused service, acting as mobile nuisances. Each targeted lunchcounter received a predetermined number of protestors. Six shortwave radios were used to coordinate activities; Ernest Brown, a Morehouse junior, operated the central radio in the church headquarters.[4] Pickets were given laminated signs so their messages would not be damaged by rain. Girls were given hooded football coats to protect them from projectiles thrown by angry whites.[5]

Using these methods the students were able to crowd Atlanta jails, create a large nuisance for the downtown businessmen, and force Mayor Hartsfield to seek a truce between the students and downtown businessmen.

Over the weekend, beginning Saturday, October 22, Mayor Hartsfield negotiated with the Student-Liaison Committee and agreed to release the students already in jail; in return, the students were to cease demonstrating for thirty days while Hartsfield acted as mediator between the students and businessmen. Rev. King was to remain in jail and face the charges brought against him. King was subsequently sentenced to four months at hard labor at Reidsville State Prison for violation of probation on a traffic charge.

At that point, events occurred to help fulfill Lonnie King's and Herschelle Sullivan's plan to affect the 1960 presidential campaign. Senator John Kennedy called M. L. King's wife, Coretta, and assured her he would do what he could to insure her husband's safety; Robert Kennedy called the judge in M. L. King's case and asked that he review the case and consider leniency. Rev. Martin Luther King, Sr., a Nixon supporter in the presidential campaign, then threw his support to the Kennedy candidacy. The most astute historians of the Kennedy administration attribute Kennedy's close victory to the black votes he received after his gesture on behalf of M. L. King, Jr. If so, Lonnie King and Herschelle Sullivan were successful in influencing the presidential campaign as they had hoped.[6]

The truce of late October did not produce a settlement and students resumed sit-ins on November 25 after the truce had been extended two days on November 22. No arrests were made during these demonstrations. Sit-ins continued through December with most department, drug, and dime stores closing lunchcounters or restaurants or just providing standup or take-out service.[7]

During January, 1961 the students slowed their activities because of final exams, reducing picketing to Fridays and Saturdays with only occasional sit-ins, while the boycott continued.[8] On February 7, 1961 seventeen students were arrested at a Sprayberry's lunchcounter, the first arrests since October.[9] On February 8 thirteen more students were arrested.[10] Then thirty-nine more were arrested on February 9.[11] February 10 brought ten more arrests, together with the report that the Fulton County Courthouse jail was overcrowded.[12]

At this point Colonel A. T. Walden, a prominent black attorney, offered his services as negotiator to the students at a meeting of black leaders on February 15. Colonel Walden went to Robert Troutman, a white attorney with connections to Rich's department store, and the two of them brought together the downtown businessmen and the Student-Adult Liaison Committee. Throughout the sit-in protests, the students had insisted on immediate desegregation of downtown lunchcounters, but the downtown businessmen had refused this change until public schools were desegregated in the fall of 1961. In return for this delayed desegregation the students would cease sit-ins, pickets, and call off the boycott. The students' position was reflected in the words of Julian Bond in the *Atlanta Inquirer*, where he wrote: "It does seem . . . that the time for action is now. Waiting for public school desegregation is like waiting for this year to roll around again. The accommodationists and the settle-for-lessers are willing to do just that."[13]

In the Troutman-Walden meeting of the opposing sides the student representatives, Lonnie King and Herschelle Sullivan initially remained adamant, refusing to accept desegregation in the fall of 1961 during the school desegregation. In the meeting they were pressured to accept desegregation "no later than October 15, 1961." Announcement of the agreement was made on March 6, but significantly no mention was made of the October 15 deadline. When the settlement was announced many students and their supporters expressed shock and dismay, since the agreement was substantially what had been proposed by the downtown businessmen since the summer of 1960.[14]

Lonnie King remembered: "We went back to the campus [that afternoon] and I gave the report to the kids, and Herschelle and I cried, and I resigned and Herschelle resigned. Because the kids did not want to accept them [terms of the agreement]."[15] Their resignations were refused, and they remained chairman and co-chair of the COAHR. Newspaper reports suggested that the students were, for the most part, against the agreement because no definite date had been announced for desegregation while most adults were for the agreement.[16]

The tension between the adults and the students over the disagreement, whether to accept or reject the settlement, came to a head at a mass meeting held at the Warren Memorial Church on March 10. Alton Hornsby recalls:

> Lonnie [King] and the students were on stage as well as the adult leadership—Walden and Martin Luther King, Sr. [etc.] So, the outline, the package . . . all seemed, sounded, fairly well except this [desegregation] would take place in the fall.
>
> And that's where the fat was thrown into the fire . . . And these were cries of 'No, no, no!!! . . . We've gone from sit-ins to sell-outs.'
>
> So, it became rather disruptive . . . And each member of the adult [leadership] tried to speak. Walden . . . continuously repeated that we are going to get this desegregation . . . he laid his life on the line for it . . . in the fall. Martin Luther King, Sr . . . the same thing—pleading for acceptance of the agreement. It just didn't go over.
>
> The only thing that saved it and pretty much stopped the revolt was when Martin Luther King, Jr. came to the church and pleaded for calm and pretty

much . . . pleaded for acceptance of the agreement . . . Now, that didn't stop the division.[17]

Although the division was not entirely healed, Dr. King's appeal did prevent the resolution from being scrapped. His appeal to the students said in part:

We must move out on the road of calm reasonableness. We must come to a mood of mutual trust and mutual confidence. No greater danger exists for the Negro community than to be afflicted with the cancerous disease of disunity. Disagreements and differences there will be, but unity there must be.[18]

The *Atlanta Inquirer* was able to report on March 18 that there were some indications that support for the resolution was growing except for the abandonment of the boycott before desegregation. No more mass sit-ins took place, although the students did seek a concrete timetable for desegregation of the lunchcounters, as rumors persisted that sit-ins would be reinstituted. The lunchcounters were finally desegregated on September 28, 1961.[19]

In discussing the sit-ins some attention must be paid to the effect that day-to-day organizing activities had on the students. There is no doubt that most involved students felt as if they had contributed to their city, their people, and their society in no small way. They took pride in what they had accomplished. Still, some individuals felt that they needed a break from the sit-in atmosphere. One such person was Mary Ann Smith Wilson, who confessed:

I had become saturated with the whole movement. It was like I was beginning to close in on myself. I knew that I needed to get out of it . . . not to get out of the movement but to open myself again . . .

During the spring of 1960 Wilson had applied for received a fellowship to the University of California at Berkeley. She explained:

I had done something I felt very good about and knew there were others who would carry on once I left . . . At that point I felt totally saturated . . . I really didn't want to stay in Atlanta. I had no qualms about leaving.[20]

Lonnie King was disappointed in how many of the adult leadership had performed during the conflict:

I was so disillusioned by the thing . . . I decided to go to school at Howard 'cause I had seen people that I had respect for all my life crumble when faced with an awesome decision. I just didn't think I could take it any more, to be quite honest with you.[21]

Thus it was that desegregation came to downtown Atlanta after eighteen months of struggle. Neither the city nor many of the people would be the same. Egos and ideals were both boosted and bruised while *de jure* segregation was dealt a blow from which it would never recover.

FOUR

"Something We Feel We Got To Do"

In view of the type and level of organizing that the Atlanta sit-in students were involved in, one must ask the question of how the sit-ins affected the personal lives of the students. How did the student protestors cope with being actively involved in organizing while at the same time fulfilling their basic purpose of being in school, that is, attending classes, studying, and making the best grades possible in preparing for life after college? Also, how did the sit-in activity of some students affect their relations with their parents? The competing demands of academic life, parents, and protest became most acute when the students were arrested and elected to stay in jail, refusing bail to emphasize their protest.

Mary Ann Smith Wilson had this to say about the degree of concern for academics on the part of students:

> As the weeks rolled on most of us got so totally involved in that [protesting] . . . I suppose toward the end of the [school] year you began to think and perhaps some people dropped classes.
> They would spend a lot of extra time trying to get it together at the end, but during the time of the peak of the movement everybody was just totally involved in it.[1]

An observer of the sit-in students commented that not even "the possibility of failure in academic classes can still the ardor of the keyed up student protestors,"[2] a judgment supported by Wilson's testimony. Lonnie King expressed similar sentiments:

> I never really worried about academics. I wasn't trying to graduate with honors. Although I did make honor roll a couple of times over there. I just decided to prove I could do it.

145

> I never really worried that much about academics in that I really thought I had the abilities to do it [protest and perform well academically]. And never worried about it that much.[3]

Even though the devotion of the students was substantial, one professor, Dr. Lois Moreland of Spelman, recalls that some students did face an "academic fear" since there was a question among some faculty members and administrators as to whether "the students should even do what they were doing."[4]

For their part the college presidents and faculty members were adamant in their belief that academic standards at the Atlanta University Center schools should not be sacrificed because of the organizing efforts in which the students were involved. Dr. Mays told the students: "You're not going to get your lessons."[5] Wendell Whalum, professor of music at Morehouse, said: "The student government was made aware by President Mays and, as I recall, Dean Brailsford Brazeal, that their [student's] studies were not to suffer in the face of their fight for human rights, for human equality. That Morehouse had always taken the lead in this and we wouldn't give it up. But Morehouse had taken the lead while training students."[6]

On the Clark campus President James Brawley was just as concerned with letting his students know he expected them to take care of their studies first before boycotts, picketing, or any other protest. He discussed how he let the students know this. He would not allow "a disruption of the educational process. We said 'if you go to jail, we'll understand but classes are going to go on.' When it was asked if classes could be dismissed so more students could participate in the demonstrations, they were told 'no, that would defeat what you are attempting to do, that we would not dismiss classes. But, what you do, you would have to do at your own risk.'" He went on to say that they, the college presidents, would try to protect the demonstrators and get them out of jail if arrested "but the educative process must go on."[7]

It appears that at all the Center schools this attitude was maintained. However much the professors and presidents on the campuses supported the students in their endeavors, they all agreed that the students should study and protest, not protest in lieu of studying. This is not to say that students were not the recipients of much understanding and consideration in their situation; on the contrary, as it developed, allowances, when needed, were given. The respondents, many times, emphasized that allowances were given "not to lower standards" but rather "to make it easier" to make up work they might have missed.[8] This took form of tutoring sessions, rescheduling examinations, and oral examinations.

The student informants varied in their testimony about allowances for sit-in students. Julian Bond saw it mainly as a scheduling problem: "If you couldn't come to class on this day to be able to take the test on the weekend or something."[9] Carolyn Long said, "while we were in jail we had books and things brought us and studied while we were there." In October of 1960, while in jail with the other students arrested in the sit-ins, Carolyn and her sister Wilma wrote that although their professors might be surprised they were "planning to send out for more books." They went on to say they were requesting the volumes not only to "keep up" with their studies but also to diminish the tedium of imprisonment. Long, in her interview said that when they were not in jail "we never missed classes. It was a matter of everything [such as] . . . planning taking place at night."[10]

Not all the students could take such a positive view of their situation as Long did in October, 1960. Some students were afraid a whole semester might be lost in jail. One writer suggested that this fear heightened the anxiousness of the students in their quest for a resolution to the conflict over desegregation.[11]

Lonnie King in his assessment leans toward Long's views in deemphasizing the necessity of allowances. "You didn't get a lot of allowances though at Morehouse . . . The only allowances we got at Morehouse—the major allowance—was in being excused from chapel. You could miss so many [classes] and they'll put you in demerits."[12]

It appears, most likely, that despite what King contends, Morehouse was not all that much different from other Center schools in this respect. Another student at Morehouse maintained "even the more conservative ones [professors] did show a certain amount of leniency. I mean, in certain instances . . . there was nothing else to do" such as "on the day when most of us marched [May 17, 1960] . . . there were no classes to meet." He added that "on many days you'd go in class and one-fourth of the people would be out and things would go on as best they could."[13]

What the students did not know or remember was that at Morehouse Dr. Mays made it official policy of the school that faculty members would make allowances for involved students. He remembered: "My faculty wasn't quite with me on my stand on that. They were not wholly in my corner. They thought that they should make that decision whether they should be a part of this thing. Well, I didn't think so. I believed that the head of the college [should] . . . and I didn't think it was a faculty matter. I had to take a stand." As time passed he believed his faculty became more amenable to his policies.[14]

At Clark, President Brawley believed "all of them [faculty] made allowances." The Clark students were told he felt "all the teachers will understand and give you an opportunity to make up the work."[5] Dr. Harry V. Richardson, President of the Interdenominational Theological Center in 1960, agreed that students were "given an opportunity to make up work where they were out in these [protest] activities . . . We did, in a number of cases, give students an opportunity to make up for time they spent in these movements."[16]

Dr. Margaret Rowley, professor at Morris Brown in 1960, detailed some of the things that were done to help the students. If a student was in jail assignments would be sent to him or her. Make-up tests or incompletes were given instead of failing marks. She was surprised that "very few" of them took advantage of the situation. "They may have missed things but most of them made it up later. They didn't use this as an excuse."[17] Mary Ann Smith Wilson, in agreement with Dr. Rowley's comments, was sure that she received some allowances because "I must have missed a lot of classes, and I was able to make up without asking for a lot of allowances. So, I'm not sure what happened in other instances." She found that professors "didn't put the pressure on" to make her decide which part of her life was most important—school work or the movement. There was one instance when she was concerned about getting a "C" grade in a course when she needed a higher grade to retain her academic scholarship while at Morris Brown, but she was able to get the grade she needed to retain her scholarship.[18]

Finally, at Spelman College, Lois Moreland was very close to the students active in the movement. She gave tutoring sessions "all the time" to help students catch up, but "there was opposition within the faculty" about such methods. She would visit the students' dormitories, and "we'd talk about the courses. I would try to make sure that they were not behind [in their classes]." Also, "if I found that most of the class was missing on a particular day an exam was scheduled, I would reschedule the exam. I wasn't punitive in any way."[19]

Dr. Clarence A. Bacote, Professor of History at A.U., who taught one course at Spelman at the time of the sit-ins, told of one student and her commitment to the struggle. The student was Ruby Doris Smith.

When I discovered her sincerity, I decided a young woman like this deserves all of the help you can give her. So, what I did was to have conferences with her. I would give special tutoring. Tell her what she missed and suggesting things she should read.[20]

She was also given oral tests and many absences were overlooked.

The students themselves had to work their schedules so that the demonstrations and jailings would not devastate their academic endeavors. Near the end of the fall semester in January, 1960, picketing was cut back to accommodate final examination schedules. Class attendance was also taken into consideration, as the number of pickets on a particular day was determined on the basis of class schedules as well as the "day's [protest] objectives."[21]

Through these different methods most of the sit-in students were able to remain in good standing academically, but a small minority, in Lonnie King's terms, became "academic casualties." He commented:

A lot of us though, actually, dropped out so we wouldn't have that kind of burden. It was a conflict trying to score on the exams, at the same time fight folks downtown.

There are some people who dropped out who have never gotten it back together. There are some casualties in the movement.[22]

One such casualty was Julian Bond:

Well, we tried. You'd try for a long time to balance school work and this kind of work [protest]. It was something I couldn't balance.

I had to give one up. I gave up the school work. Most people tried. Some people suffered.[23]

If it was difficult for some students to handle the responsibilities of tending to studies while protesting, there can be no doubt that many students agonized over the dilemma of possibly incurring the disfavor of their parents by sitting in. Parents feared for their children's safety, economic reprisals, and damage to status.

Lonnie King was married and had a family of his own while attending Morehouse but knew well the pressures involved in parent-student conflict over involvement in the direct action movement. One student at Morehouse, Joe Pierce, had an aunt who was a school teacher: "[she] felt that he was going to get her fired."[24] Pierce was able to remain active but others were not. "After it [sit-ins and arrests] happened," Julian Bond recalled, "One or two students were forbidden to have anything to do with this again." Those parents argued. "I sent you to Morehouse and you come back with a police record. It's too much. But this was the exception, not the rule."[25]

Carolyn Long remembers that "some" parents were supportive of their children's sit-in activities to a "certain extent." Her comments echo those of Bond:

> . . . When it got to the point of arrests they didn't want them to be involved at all. Because the main thing, you know, professional blacks in Atlanta were thinking of is, 'You're gonna ruin your career for the future and you'll have a record and we worked too hard putting you through college for you to just throw it away.' That kind of thing.
>
> I really wouldn't want to call any names. There were some [students] who confided in us that their parents had told them that if they got that involved [to the point of being arrested], then they wouldn't have anyplace to stay and that kind of thing. But, that was in the minority.[26]

It is probably true that most parents of student activists did not prohibit their daughters and sons from participating in the sit-ins. It is also likely that most were not enthusiastic in their support for their children. The majority were only marginally instrumental in determining whether or not their children were involved in protest activity. In some instances, parents tried to dissuade their offspring from participating in demonstrations where violence was always imminent but acquiesced when the young woman or man communicated just how dedicated he or she was to the movement. In other instances, parents did not express sentiments overtly but gave tacit support.

Mary Ann Smith Wilson and her sister, Ruby Doris Smith,—the former at Morris Brown and the latter at Spelman—were both committed members of the Atlanta Student movement from its initial states. Their parents gave quiet support to their daughters. "They definitely did not speak out or prohibit me or my sister from participating at all," said Wilson. "I'm pretty sure there were some things they couldn't understand about it but, I think, ultimately they felt there was nothing but good that could come out of that kind of thing. So, for the most part they were very supportive." When asked if they communicated their support openly she replied by saying: "No, it was very subtle, very subtle. There was no open [message] that 'you have my support, go ahead and do your thing.' But there was no objection of what we felt we had to do."[27]

The student who took credit for recruiting the two sisters into the movement recalled the reluctance of the two sisters' mother. Mrs. Smith told him. "You've got both of my girls in this thing and I hope it works out."[28] Another parent who feared for the well being of his daughter but allowed her to participate, was a Professor of Theology at Morehouse, Roswell F. Jackson. He "reluctantly" gave his daughter permission to sit-in. Why was he reluctant? "The only true answer is that I feared for her safety." He saw this as a "selfish" concern common to "middle-class blacks," who were "generally afraid" of challenging the white racist system. His daughter told him that becoming a part of the movement was "something she had to do" and would sit-in with or without her parents' permission. Although he was doubtful as to the possibility of success that the students would have in desegregating the downtown lunchcounters and other facilities, he felt something "needed to be done." He admired "those who had courage and conviction" because "I had been a victim of the situation for years."[29]

Alton Hornsby's discussion with his mother was similar to that of Roswell Jackson's with his daughter. He recounted:

> . . . When my mother and I got around to talking about it . . . she didn't prohibit me but advised me not to get, you know, deeply involved in it.
>
> I replied, I guess, as most replied, at the time, that this was something we were going to have to do. I didn't use these words, meaning no disrespect and anything of that nature: 'This was something we feel we got to do.'[30]

In addition to those parents who were either nonsupportive or who found that their children's commitment was too strong to overcome, there were others who were more openly supportive. Most prominent among these was Ralph Long, father of Carolyn and Wilma Long, both students at Clark college and members of the student movement. In his position as head of the Atlanta Student Defense Fund, organized to provide bail money for those arrested, Long placed himself on the front lines in support of the students for justice, serving as a bondsman. He describes his contribution in this way:

> We had to have, after they got arrested, we had to have people to bond them out . . . I volunteered to be a bondsman because of my children and so many other[s].
>
> I knew it was the right thing to do and so many of the adults in Atlanta refused to do it . . . I just took it on my own. I was responsible for $100,000 and that is what I signed up for . . . against my property.

From the beginning, Mr. Long said, "They had my blessings all the way . . . my daughters . . . I wish that it had been possible to have done this years before."[31]

Long was principal of the John Hope Elementary School in 1960, and concern was expressed by some to his children that his activities in the student movement might jeopardize his career.

> I remember one time someone suggested to them [his children] that they not do this because it would jeopardize my job, and they came to me and we talked about it and what not.
>
> I said, 'I'm a man of my convictions.' If they wanted to continue to do it, they should go ahead and do it. I told them 'You don't have to hide behind anything.'

Long told the superintendent of schools that he was involved in work for the student movement. She did not interfere and asked only that he keep her informed of time he had to spend away from his school. Some of his co-workers were critical of his involvement and reported it to the school superintendent, whereupon she called a meeting of her staff telling them she knew of Long's involvement in the student movement and that she found nothing wrong with Long's activity; moreover, she admonished them that she thought very little of those who felt it necessary to report Long's activities.[32]

Mrs. Ralph Long also was concerned with the student movement. For her part, Mrs. Long was not "surprised" when the sit-ins began in Atlanta since they had first occurred in North Carolina. At the time of the March 15 demonstrations in Atlanta, she and other parents "settled down to waiting until the fad exhausted itself." When her daughters were arrested later in 1960 during the fall campaign against segregation, she "wept tears of frustration in the middle of the night, when my own daughters deliberately put themselves out of reach, behind locked doors, through which I could not follow."

That night she was somewhat "jealous" of the movement, she recounted, because it "so radically disturbed and changed the pattern of our home life as we had known it, as we so desperately wished it could be." Religion helped her to bear the strains better. More than a year after the sit-ins began and after the resolution to the conflict had been reached, she felt that the student movement was something she wanted to "wait for me" as opposed to being left behind in its struggle for equality.[33] Another parent, Lee

Brown, father of Ben Brown of Clark, also spoke of religion in relation to the movement. He felt "the children are doing God's work."[34]

The parents of Julian Bond were like those of the Long sisters. Bond's father, Horace Mann Bond, was a well-known educator, college president, and activist, in his own right. Julian considered both his parents "very supportive. They were surprised, but I don't think either . . . thought it was anything 'bad.'"[35] But, initially, at least, Mrs. Bond admitted to being against her son's involvement. She has said, ". . . most people like us were opposed to it."[36] Another author maintains that Bond's parents "had reservations about the student movement, to begin with" and "came to accept it."[37] There can be no doubt that Mrs. Bond was alarmed when Julian Bond was arrested in the March 15 sit-ins. When Julian's father arrived home the evening of March 15 after Julian and the other students had been arrested, Mrs. Bond shouted to her husband as he walked to the door: "Julian's got arrested!"[38] Even though the Bonds became like those parents who either quietly or more openly supported their children in the student movement; still, the great majority of parents did not influence their children's participation.

FIVE

"I Had To Be With Them"

Besides the students' parents probably no group considered themselves more responsible for what they considered the well-being of the students than the presidents of the six A.U.C. schools. In 1960 the presidents and their respective schools were: Dr. Rufus Clement, Atlanta University, who was also president of the Council of Presidents; Dr. Benjamin E. Mays, Morehouse; Dr. James Brawley, Clark; Dr. Harry V. Richardson, Interdenominational Theological Center; Dr. Albert Manley, Spelman; and Dr. James Cunningham, Morris Brown. For this study Richardson, Brawley, and Mays were interviewed.

All of the presidents interviewed emphasized their support of the student movement; nevertheless, while supporting the students, the presidents had to take many things into account, the first of which was that of legal responsibility for the safety of the students.[1] Besides legal considerations, the presidents no doubt, were conscious of other pressures that could be brought to bear on colleges. Dr. Mays "politely refused" the request of one trustee of Morehouse that he prevent the students from demonstrating.[2] In addition, all of the presidents had been affected by discrimination themselves, making it very difficult for them, as individuals, to oppose action on the students' part to desegregate downtown lunchcounters. On the other hand one interviewer of Atlanta student activists has written that the presidents "urged on the students a plan which spared the downtown merchants, some of whom were financial supporters of the college."[3] In effect, the presidents were motivated by conflicting impulses which influenced them to take actions, at certain times, favorable to change and, at other times, restrain, delay and even stifle methods the students used to break the color line in downtown Atlanta.

Soon after the Greensboro sit-ins, the A.U.C. presidents became aware A.U.C. students were planning sit-ins of their own. According to Brawley, "that was knowledge that was pretty widely available when the first sit-ins began in North Carolina at A and T College. From that particular time on we were very much aware of what was going on . . . We knew they were going to get into the act and we encouraged them to."[4] He continued:

> We encouraged them, because we [the presidents] knew the best way to handle a situation of this kind was to assure the students we were sympathetic that we were as much interested in what they were doing to bring about change as they were. And we knew it would be most effective if we could work together, instead of working against one another.[5]

The response of Richardson was similar:

> The general feeling among the presidents was that this was a justifiable cause, that the students were taking part in the push for civil rights, to break down Southern segregation from which we all had suffered.
> This was the students' effort . . . to bear witness and take a part in it. I know that as far as possible we all were sympathetic to it. I do remember we had two or three sessions in which to discuss this.[6]

From the interviews conducted it appears that the presidents met among themselves, initially, to discuss the situation. Then, as demonstrations appeared imminent, they called the student protest leaders in to discuss plans for demonstrations in February of 1960.

It is important to note that the students felt a need to keep their plans away from the presidents and adults as much as possible for fear they would try to stop the students' efforts. Julian Bond commented that the students tried to discuss their plans as little as possible with adults.[7] The students kept the members of the Student-Adult Liaison Committee, many of whom were businessmen with contacts in the white community, designed to facilitate adult support work, at arms' length, even though the adults in it could be considered devoted in their support of the students. The adults in the committee were not allowed in the students' policy and strategy meetings but were asked by the students to "serve in an advisory capacity." This was because "we preferred not to embarrass or otherwise discompose our adult leadership; they may have vested interests or personal obligations which may make it more difficult for them to share directly in our deliberations, or in our strategy and the implementation."[8] This arm's length attitude was also true for the college presidents.

When the presidents did find out that the students were organizing demonstrations they called in the student protest leaders and many of those who had been organized.[9]

Lonnie King related this:

The Council of . . . Presidents got wind of what was going on and Dr. Mays sent Mrs. Hill, who was his secretary to the corner [at Yates and Milton Drugstore] one day to get me and Joe [Pierce] and Julian [Bond].

He summoned us to a room we didn't know existed—this big, ornate, conference room. When we all got there, there were all these students we had been organizing. [Laughter] I said, 'Lord, I must be out of school now.' [Laughter]

So, anyway, we came in. They [presidents] told me about the fact that they had heard what we were doing, and that they were concerned about it. They gave us a lecture about their responsibilities as college presidents to not get the students killed . . . They had a responsibility to the students.

It was really imposing. And everyone looked at me [as if to say] 'Speak, leader.' So, I told them that I basically shared their concerns and I was concerned about that too. But, I thought we had a broader concern and that was the shackles of segregation and discrimination and if we were going to make this wall fall we needed to join in now. We were prepared to do all that. I talked about our responsibilities as human beings.[10]

At this point, Dr. Clement proposed an option to sit-ins. He suggested the students let a legal challenge be attempted by the NAACP. "We basically said if we tried it from a legal point of view . . . it would take a long time."[11]

Ms. Wilson's recollections of one such meeting called by the presidents to influence the students' actions substantiates King's account. "The feeling [of the presidents] was, sure, Atlanta had all the problems of segregation, but let's try to do something in a more constructive way. We can make some contacts. We can initiate some contacts downtown. I think probably the presidents were concerned that the campus just didn't become totally disrupted behind this."[12]

The "constructive" action Clement proposed in early March, after the option of legal maneuvering was rejected, was the writing of a statement of grievances by the students to let the public know why they were protesting. On the Appeal for Human Rights, Julian Bond said: "He [Clement] . . . was helpful in a way he didn't intend to be. He said 'if you do this, if you have this and demonstrate, no one will know why.' Of course, everybody would know why, we wanted to eat at the damned lunchcounters. He said 'why don't you issue a statement explaining why you were doing it.' I think he was trying to delay it, but we drafted this statement called "An Appeal for Human Rights."[13]

Lonnie King remembers that after it was understood that the students would take to the streets:

> Clement recommended that we the students, and I'm sure that was their united recommendation—he was just saying it—that we write an Appeal for Human Rights and put it in the newspapers.
>   Clement advanced it [the money] from A.U. at first, but they raised money from all over America. In other words we were the best financed of any [sit-in] group.[14]

Julian Bond felt that "in retrospect [Clement's proposal] was a delaying move . . . what Dr. Clement really wanted to do was have us put off the initial demonstrations, believing if we ever did begin we couldn't be stopped."[15] If that was Clement's intention, he was successful only in delaying, not stopping the sit-ins from taking place. The first sit-ins engineered by the group summoned to the meeting with the college presidents did not occur until March 15 in the middle of the month after the students began organizing in early February. Even the agreement between the presidents and the students about writing an appeal was not "unanimous at first. There were those who felt we should be out there doing what all the other students were doing," said Wilson.[16] Finally a compromise was struck with the understanding that the publishing of an appeal did not preclude demonstrations.

It was further agreed that the first demonstrations would be a test case to reveal the grievances of the students and provide a court case. The students found themselves, Lonnie King remembers, "running with the foxes and chasing with the hounds on that issue. We tried to satisfy the college presidents but at the same time carry this thing through."[17]

At different times the reservations of the presidents were communicated to the students. Dr. Richardson confided that "where students were making unwise efforts, I think we would advise them against it." They were counseled not to indulge in activity which was either "too radical or for which they were legally liable." Richardson asserted that the presidents "on a number of occasions when the students would make their reports, we would . . . caution them about certain activities because we just thought it was overexposure on them . . . I do know there were many cases, a number of cases where we felt the students were unwise," although they never told the students not to participate in protest activities.[18] At one point the presidents did prohibit students from meeting with sympathetic white college students at the A.U.C.[19] In addition, both Brawley and Mays recalled they admonished the students that they should tell their parents of their plans to sit-in.

The meetings between the presidents and the students continued irregularly for a while in 1960, according to Julian Bond. The presidents in those meetings, Bond said, tried to say "why don't you young people come in here, tell us what you're going to do . . . before it happens. We don't want to be taken off guard. You see when we got arrested we didn't tell anybody."[20] This last statement is most likely not accurate. Dr. Mays, in his autobiography, maintains that at midnight the night before the first Atlanta sit-ins of March 15, "A group of students visited my residence to inform me that demonstrations were on."[21] This does not appear to be the case for the other presidents in the A.U.C.

When the students were planning to march on the state capitol on May 17, 1960, the presidents were in touch with Atlanta police chief Herbert Jenkins and Mayor William Hartsfield who asked them to try to stop the students from marching to the state capitol during their march on the way to the rally at Wheat Street Baptist Church on Auburn Avenue. Dr. Mays spoke to King:

> I remember when I told [Lonnie] King . . . [what Jenkins and Hartsfield said]. He said he had to go back to his committee.
> Then they came back and assembled and King made a beautiful speech. He said 'If there is anybody in here that's going to be violent, don't go. If anybody can't go to jail without fighting he's not for this!' Nobody, nobody dropped out. No . . . not a single one.
> Then, I knew that it [the movement] couldn't be stopped and I wasn't going to try. Because here are these kids doing what I wasn't going to try. Because here are these kids doing what I had been doing alone since the turn of the century—fighting against injustice, discrimination . . .
> So, I couldn't say to these students they couldn't do what I had been doing alone. I'd been almost lynched three times . . . I was, of course, I had to be with them.[22]

About this incident Lonnie King recalled:

> Dr. Mays and all of them called me in and asked me to call off the march. I told them I couldn't do it. I said 'you all have been teaching us that we have

to become leaders. So, now that we have an opportunity to be leaders today, you don't tell us to be leaders tomorrow. We have a chance to be leaders today and I think we ought to do it, and we are ready.'

I prayed and went on. Dr. Mays and his wife, Miss Sadie—they all said 'Son, we all hope things come out all right.'[23]

As the students approached the capitol, Jenkins personally ordered Lonnie King to divert the march threatening him with arrest if he did not do so. King obeyed the order, basing his decision on the fear of what would happen to the movement he had done so much to organize. "See, I didn't want to give the college presidents a stick to beat me over the head with." It was a stick he was sure they would use.[24]

Even in view of this, King was able to say "all the college presidents were supportive of us intellectually, but as a practical matter, at the very outset of the movement, they thought we were going a little too fast.[25] This was the presidents' dilemma: there were times they took actions which seemed to show they were for the movement and at other times took actions that seemed to show they were not for the movement. As has been said, they once prohibited interracial meetings of students on campus after the sit-ins had started. Another time they met with a group of white businessmen to ask them to desegregate their businesses to forestall the need for further demonstrations. One businessman told them desegregation would never come to Atlanta. Dr. Mays told him dryly, "Never is a long time."[26]

Dr. Brawley had a chance to tell another of the downtown businessmen his views when the businessman suggested that the presidents stop the students from demonstrating. Brawley replied:

We can't stop these students. This is a movement. You've got to understand that this is a movement and it's not only a movement on any particular campus . . . but it's a movement nationwide. That you can't stop a movement of that kind. That this is a revolution.

. . . They told you what they want. There's nothing else and nothing short of compliance on the part of the white people here in Atlanta.

You've got to open up these stores, you've got to open up these restaurants, you've got to open up these lunchcounters so that there'll be no discrimination. No more segregation and that sort of thing.

He summed up his comments by saying "Well, it was a hard job to do, but they did it."[27]

Over a period of time the college presidents did come out publicly in support of the students. By the time of commencement in May, 1960, Dr.

Albert Manley was able to tell the graduating class at Spelman: " . . . just as we [adults] had settled back and begun to believe your generation was indifferent to the great social issues of the day, you surprised all of us."[28] Dr. Richardson wrote an eloquent article in 1962 detailing his support for the student sit-in movement from a theological perspective.[29]

If the presidents found themselves in a paradoxical position, their faculty members were more able to take clearer positions on the student movement. Faculty members at the A.U.C. fell into three groups in relation to the student movement: those supportive of the sit-in students; those aloof from the sit-in students; and, finally, those who were against the students' methods, if not their goals. The first and last groups appear to have been in the minority; the middle group appears to have been the largest of the three.

At Spelman College, Dr. Lois Moreland, in 1960, was a lecturer in the political science department. Students active in the movement approached her for advice.

> As I recall, some students came to me to talk to me about it. We had a very close relationship. I was very young and just about the same age as my students.
>
> As I recall, some of the student leaders were in one of my classes . . . They were keeping me abreast of what they were going to do, or planning to do, or hoped to do.
>
> They were asking advice, too, because I was a political science teacher.[30]

Lonnie King and Julian Bond asked her to be the student movement's advisor, but she declined because she was pregnant at the time. She and her husband decided the risk of racist retaliation was too much of a danger to their unborn child.[31] Moreland summarized her role in the movement:

> I think the role I played was more like a counselor, not an advisor . . . they did come to me for emotional support, perhaps like a big sister. They'd talk about the concerns in the jail. They'd talk about the kinds of things they did.
>
> They wanted me to talk about the law. They wanted me to talk about existential philosophy which they were very much into at the time. They had just read Sartre, apparently.
>
> I was not a strategist for the movement, but I was supportive in the sense that anybody who is under pressure wants a sympathetic sounding board.[32]

Another supportive faculty member at Spelman was Howard Zinn, of the history department, who took an active role in helping the students. A group of students used his car to ride downtown to sit-in on March 15, and he was assigned the duty of calling the media that morning to explain the student's reasons for demonstrating. Zinn and his wife participated in a sit-in at a Rich's lunch room where each ordered two meals and seated themselves. Then black students, including King, Carolyn Long, and John Gibson joined them at which time the lunch room was closed.[33] Zinn described his relation to the Atlanta student movement as one of an "observer, a friend and an occasional participant. I had picketed supermarkets, sat-in at Rich's, gone with my students to desegregate the gallery of the legislature and marched downtown in a mass parade."[34] In his book, the *Southern Mystique*, which discussed Southern race relations in general and focused, in part, on the A.U.C. and the student movement, he dedicated the volume to his students at Spelman by saying that "without [them] . . . this book could not have been written."[35]

Dr. Wendell Whalum was an instructor of music and advisor to the Student Government Association at Morehouse when the sit-in movement broke out. He was among a group of faculty members at Morehouse who were supportive of the student movement, but at the same time, were ready to admonish the students if they perceived the student's actions to be incorrect. He explained "because of my then youthful status . . . students were a lot more communicative to me and I knew what was going on from almost the very beginning of the movement."[36] In more detail Whalum described how a group of professors came close to the movement:

> He [Dr. Mays] asked Dr. [Robert] Brisbane, Mr. [William] Nix who was the Director of Personnel . . . then . . . and he asked a couple of other teachers . . . one was the late Dr. Sam Williams and he asked me . . . to . . . come to a meeting with the student government heads where he made it clear that we should help the students articulate what they were trying to do.[37]

Dr. Robert Brisbane of the political science department probably became, along with Dr. Sam Williams, the closest Morehouse faculty member to the student movement. Brisbane's research specialty was black protest and fourteen years later in his book, *Black Activism*, a history of the recent black protest movement, he wrote of the Atlanta student movement he advised.[38] Dr. Whalum had this to say on Brisbane:

> I do remember this well. Brisbane let us know that he really didn't need any help. That he and Sam Williams and Nix could touch base if they had to...[39]

Williams, head of Morehouse's philosophy department and pastor of the influential Friendship Baptist Church, preached "these students who are acting . . . God bless them. They are separating the men from the boys." At a protest meeting he went further and told the assemblage: "We're going to stay with, and even die with the students if necessary."[40] Dr. Lionel Newsom in the sociology department at Morehouse was another faculty member that gave support to the students.[41]

At Clark, M. Carl Holman was cited as the faculty member at that school most dedicated to the movement. He was the student movement's second advisor, helped the students begin the *Atlanta Inquirer* newspaper, and became its editor.[42] Holman's comments in a March, 1961 editorial at the time of the sit-in agreement between the students and businessmen is indicative of the tone he contributed to the movement. He believed the settlement was a matter of "treason and heresy" by the black adults who had pressured the students into accepting the agreement. He criticized anyone who saw the settlement as a "major victory."[43]

At Atlanta University Whitney Young, Dean of the School of Social Work, was clearly on the side of the student movement as its first faculty advisor. In a town meeting held at the university in the spring of 1960, Young spoke of the four values the sit-ins had. They had "dramatized injustice," "fought apathy," "released hostility," and "secured action."[44] Tilman C. Cothran, a professor in the School of Social Work expressed a perceptive attitude supportive of the student movement. Cothran in July, 1960 addressed a summer school assembly saying "Negro young people have lost their patience and are trying to change a world they didn't create."[45]

Although no faculty member at Morris Brown and ITC appears to have been as active and vocal as those at the other schools they nonetheless did support their students. In a human relations program at Morris Brown, Dr. Margaret Rowley and other staff members had a vehicle through which they were able to contribute. She said:

> I saw my part as a technician [in the human relations program]. We taught people about change and what it means and how you bring it about . . . I thought my role was as supportive and helping with education . . . not just vague education but for the task they had to do.[46]

The number of openly non-supportive faculty members was small. Whalum said: "I can tell you that there was a divided group" with one group of older teachers "who said they're doing too much, they [students] need to withdraw," or slow down their protest activities. On Spelman's campus Lois Moreland did observe "opposition within the faculty" to the student movement in the initial stages of the movement.[47]

At some points, the students experienced problems with professors who felt they should stay out of the movement. Alton Hornsby had three faculty advisors while at Morehouse, one the chairman of the History Department, Hornsby's major area of study, the other two advisors in his minor areas of concentration, German and education. He summarized their stance:

> Some were downright opposed. The history chairman, and this caused me great concern, advised me personally not to get involved, saying what I was going to risk in terms of scholarships and future careers.

The advisor in the German department was also against his involvement, while Dr. D. L. Boger, the third advisor, voiced his support in no uncertain terms.[48]

Carolyn Long's French teacher at Clark, a white man, gave "very, very long dissertations on why blacks should stay in their places." She "wondered why he never spoke to me or called on me in class and so forth." The semester she took his class in conversational French she received a grade of "D." The next semester, at Morris Brown, she took another class in French and received an "A."[49]

Arthur C. Banks, Jr., a professor in Morehouse's Political Science department, was more moderate in his opposition to the student movement, although he made it clear that picketing was not the best thing the students could have been doing with their time in college. In a letter to the *Nation*, in reply to a previous article by Spelman professor Howard Zinn, Banks said that although the students' efforts were for a "noble cause" the demonstrations "may have been carried on at the expense of legitimate classroom activity. It would be helpful indeed if these picketing energies were used to strengthen and intensify intellectual activity on the Negro college campus . . . Carrying picket signs is good exercise, but reading Great Books can yield greater profits."[50]

The greater part of the faculty in the A.U.C. did not voice an open opinion either for or against the student movement. Hornsby said "that most of the faculty here at Morehouse and in the A.U.C. were simply aloof."[51] King commented "many, most of the faculty members didn't express an opinion one way or the other."[52]

As the sit-in movement extended through 1960 and 1961 faculty members became more supportive of the student movement, as did the larger black Atlanta community. In Lonnie King's words, "it [faculty attitude] got more positive. You see, in the beginning I think a lot of people including students and faculty were apprehensive," because of the dangers inherent in resisting racist discrimination in the deep South. Moreland agreed that the faculty's attitude had changed to a more supportive posture over time.[53]

Generally, then, the majority of faculty members in the A.U.C. did not actively involve themselves in helping and supporting the sit-in students. Over time, more professors expressed greater support of the students: a core of faculty members did actively support their students; a smaller group of professors fought the current of the times and tried to discourage the students from taking part in the movement.

"The Struggle is Still Going On"

Atlanta's black college students had been given an example of indigenous protest in the form of the Montgomery bus boycott. Some stayed in foreign countries for extended periods of time and saw that racial segregation was not a universal human experience. Closer to home, they saw the genuinely heroic black adolescents of the public school integration battles. Most importantly, they had been a part of many degrading personal experiences themselves in a racist society.

As a result the students had the necessary inner strength and commitment to create an indigenous mass movement for the desegregation of lunchcounters, restaurants, restrooms, and other public accommodations in Atlanta. When the students began their organizing efforts, they had most of the white South against them. The courage it took to sit-in, picket, march, and boycott in the face of the brutality the white South could dispense was honestly heroic.

It was not only the racist white South that students had to contend with. Many parents were fearful for the students' safety and the loss of their own jobs. The college presidents, while identifying with the students' goals, tried to contain and direct the students' methods, in a fashion they felt best. Faculty members were a mixed lot with some actively for the movement, fewer openly against it, and most aloof or non-involved.

The Southern student protest movement was not a first, but an important step in a continuum of black protest. It was, in another sense, unique, in that it was the first instance of mass direct action in the recent civil rights movement. It took strength from the example of the Montgomery bus boycott and gave impetus to the freedom rides, voter registration campaigns, marches, boycotts, and freedom rides that exploded onto the scene in the 1960s and 1970s.

At the same time, the sit-in movement was limited, in that it did not attack the economic effects of institutional racism. Although one might have gained the right to sit at a lunchcounter, it was another thing to be able to buy a meal at the same lunchcounter. Also, the sit-in movement of 1960 and 1961 was most effective in the upper and urban South. Many rural and deep South areas had to wait until enforcement of the 1964 Civil Rights Act for desegregation of eating facilities. These qualifications may miss the point.

The sit-in movement was a movement full of potential. That potential has been fulfilled only to a degree. The sad fact is that racism and its effects still plague the lives of black people in this country. In 1960 the time had come for an important step in the struggle against that plague. The struggle is still going on.

Notes

INTRODUCTION

1. The Atlanta student sit-in movement was treated in a fictional manner by Milton Machlin, *Atlanta* (New York: Avon Books, 1979), pp. 47-56.
2. The Atlanta University Center is a consortium of predominantly black schools in Atlanta, Georgia. Those schools are Morehouse College; Spelman College; Clark college; Morris Brown college; Atlanta University, a graduate school; and the Interdenominational Theological Center. Hereafter, it will be designated as the A.U.C.
3. John Bracey, Jr., August Meier, and Elliott Rudwick, *Conflict and Competition; Studies in the Recent Black Protest Movement* (Belmont, California: Wadsworth Publishing Company, Inc., 1971), pp. 1-4.
4. Division of the Social Sciences, Tuskegee Institute "The Tuskegee Institute Student Movement; A Sociological Analysis," Tuskegee, Alabama, May, 1960. [Mimeographed]
5. Dr. Marcellus Barksdale provided this and other valuable insights on the civil rights movement during a seminar in the fall of 1978 at Atlanta University.

CHAPTER ONE

1. Interview with Julian Bond, Georgia State Capitol, Atlanta, Georgia, 10 April 1979; Martin Luther King, Jr., *Stride Toward Freedom; The Montgomery Story* (New York: Harper and Row Publishers, 1964), passim. See James Forman, *Freedom—When?* (New York: Random House, 1965), p. 81, for comments of an Atlanta student: "I myself desegregated that lunchcounter on Peachtree Street. Nobody else. I did it by sitting-in, by walking the picket line, by marching. I didn't have to wait for any big shots to do it for me. I did it for me."
2. Interview with Julian Bond.
3. James Forman, *The Making of Black Revolutionaries* (New York: MacMillan Company, 1972), p. 85.
4. Interview with Julian Bond.
5. *Atlanta Journal*, 13 March 1960, sec B, p. 11.
6. Interview with Lonnie King, Onyx Corporation, Atlanta, Georgia, 20 April 1979.
7. Howell Raines, *My Soul is Rested: Movement Days in the Deep South Remembered* (New York: Bantam Books, Inc., 1978), p. 84.
8. Jack Walker, *Protest and Negotiation: A Study of Negro Political Leaders in a Southern City* (Ann Arbor, Mich.: University Microfilms, Inc., 1964), p. 153.

9. Charles Merrill, Jr. scholarships were fifteen month foreign travel-study grants. Merrill felt "that the United States is in need of young people with as broad an education as possible to serve the community." "Spelman College Students Receive Scholarships for Study and Travel," *Spelman Messenger*, May, 1959, p. 17.

10. Roslyn Pope and Marian Wright, "Merrill Scholars Report," *Spelman Messenger*, November, 1959, p. 6.

11. See Howard Zinn, "Finishing School for Pickets," *Nation*, August 6, 1960, pp. 71-73, for discussion of the impact of international contacts on Spelman students. This College student wrote that one factor in influencing the black students to protest was the fact "we have traveled more and we have had more contact with the world." *New York Times*, 11 April 1960, p. 30.

12. John Neary, *Julian Bond: Black Rebel* (New York: William Morrow and Company, Inc., 1971), p. 50.

13. Interview with Mary Ann Smith Wilson, Southside Community Health Center, Atlanta, Georgia, 13 April 1979.

14. Interview with Mary Ann Smith Wilson.

15. Interview with Carolyn Long, 1275 Fair Street, S.W., Atlanta, Georgia, 13 July 1979.

16. Interview with Carolyn Long. In the fall of 1962 Howard Zinn assigned a class of his at Spelman an essay in which the students were to write of their "first encounters with racial discrimination." Although this was after the phase of the movement I am dealing with, the statements by the Spelman students are relevant in that they powerfully reflect the feelings of black students in terms of confrontations with racial segregation. These incidents are similar to those discussed above. Howard Zinn, *The Southern Mystique* (New York: Alfred A. Knopf, 1974), pp. 139-141.

CHAPTER TWO

1. Raines, *My Soul Is Rested*, pp. 73-83; Robert H. Brisbane, *Black Activism; Racial Revolution in the United States, 1954-1970* (Valley Forge, Pennsylvania; Judson Press, 1974), pp. 43-45.

2. Brisbane, *Black Activism*, pp. 47-48; Raines, *My Soul Is Rested*, pp. 84-86; Benjamin E. Mays, *Born to Rebel: An Autobiography* (New York; Scribner's Sons, 1971), p. 287; C. Eric Lincoln, "Strategy of a Sit-In," *The Reporter*, July 5, 1961, pp. 20-23; Roger W. Williams, *The Bonds: An American Family* (New York: Atheneum Press, 1972), pp. 203-04; John Hope Franklin, *From Slavery to Freedom: A History of Negro Americans* (New York: Alfred A. Knopf, 1974), p. 476; Neary, *Julian Bond: Black Rebel*, pp. 53-54.

3. Howard Zinn, *SNCC: The New Abolitionists* (Boston: Beacon Press, 1964), p. 17.

4. Mays, *Born to Rebel*, p. 287; Walker, *Protest and Negotiation*, pp. 69-70.

5. Interview with Julian Bond; and interview with Lonnie King.

6. Neary, *Julian Bond: Black Rebel*, p. 53

7. Raines, *My Soul Is Rested*, p. 86.
8. Interview with Mary Ann Smith Wilson.
9. Interview with Alton Hornsby, Morehouse College, Atlanta, Georgia, 3 May 1979.
10. Interview with Alton Hornsby.
11. Interview with Carolyn Long.
12. Interview with Julian Bond.
13. Mays, *Born to Rebel*, p. 287; Walker, *Protest and Negotiation*, p. 70, gives the same reason and footnotes an interview that was probably with Lonnie King.
14. Brisbane, *Black Activism*, p. 48.
15. Interview with Julian Bond.
16. George B. Leonard, Jr., "The Second Battle of Atlanta," *Look*, April 25, 1961, p. 38.
17. Interview with Lonnie King. Howard Zinn makes the distinction of one group being more militant than the other. See Zinn, *Southern Mystique*, p. 108.
18. See *Atlanta Constitution*, 9 March 1960, p. 3. On Monday seven black students and one white person sat in at a Rich's lunchcounter and were told to leave, which they promptly did. The article said "informed sources said Tuesday that the seven were a 'maverick' group and their action was not instigated by the organized movement that exists among the city's negro college students." This group was probably the A.U. faction.
19. Interview with Lonnie King.
20. Interview with Alton Hornsby.
21. Interview with Lonnie King.
22. See *Atlanta Constitution*, 9 March 1960, p. 13; *Atlanta Journal*, 9 March 1960, pp. 1, 10, 31; *Atlanta Daily World*, 9 March 1960, p. 8. The Appeal was signed by Willie Mays, president of the A.U. Dormitory Council; James Felder, president of the student government association at Clark; Marion D. Bennet, president of the student government association at ITC; Mary Ann Smith (Wilson), secretary of the student government association at Morris Brown; and Roslyn Pope, president of the student government association at Spelman.
23. Interviews with Julian Bond and Lonnie King.
24. Interviews with Lonnie King, Julian Bond, and Carolyn Long.
25. Interview with Julian Bond; Walker, *Protest and Negotiation*, p. 74.
26. *Atlanta Constitution and Journal*, 13 March 1960, p. 11-B.
27. Interviews with Julian Bond; and Donald L. Hollowell, 1389 Peachtree Street, Atlanta, Georgia 30 November 1979; Raines, *My Soul is Rested*, pp. 87-88.
28. Neary, *Julian Bond: Black Rebel*, p. 55; Zinn, *Southern Mystique*, p. 112.
29. See interviews with Julian Bond and Donald L. Hollowell.
30. Zinn, *SNCC: The New Abolitionists*, p. 17.
31. *Atlanta Daily World*, 16 March 1960, pp. 1-2; *Atlanta Constitution*, 16 March 1960, pp. 1, 9.
32. *Atlanta Daily World*, 26 April 1960, p. 1; Lincoln, "Strategy of a Sit-In," p. 21.
33. Interview with King; *Atlanta Journal*, 16 May 1960, p. 12; See pp. 41-42 for a discussion of presidents and their reaction to the May 17 march.

34. Interview with Lonnie King; *Atlanta Daily World*, 18 May 1960, pp. 1, 4; *Atlanta Journal*, 17 May 1960, pp. 1, 9; *Atlanta Constitution*, pp. 1, 8; Walker, *Protest and Negotiation*, p. 89.

35. Interview with Mary Ann Smith Wilson.

36. Interview with Lonnie King; Lincoln, "Strategy of a Sit-In," p. 21.

37. Walker, *Protest and Negotiation*, p. 92.

38. *Ibid.*; *Atlanta Constitution*, 8 August 1960, pp. 1, 6; 15 August 1960, p. 10; 22 August 1960, p. 6.

39. *New York Times*, 4 August 1960, p. 25; *Atlanta Constitution*, 4 August 1960, pp. 1, 11.

40. Interview with Lonnie King; Raines, *My Soul is Rested*, p. 90.

41. See *Atlanta Inquirer*, 31 July 1960 to 25 March 1961; Neary, *Julian Bond: Black Rebel*, pp. 60-62; Williams, *The Bonds: An American Family*, pp. 207-08.

42. Raines, *My Soul is Rested*, p. 90; See *Atlanta Constitution*, 24 June 1960, p. 36 where King acknowledged Rich's was the first target in their domino theory; and *Atlanta Inquirer*, 12 September 1960, p. 3 where King discusses meaning of community support to the sit-in movement.

43. Raines, *My Soul is Rested*, pp. 91-93.

44. Students instrumental in the COAHR were: Fred C. Bennet, a Morris Brown pre-theology student who acted as executive director; Robert "Tex" Felder, a second-year student at the ITC was deputy chief of operations; Rev. Otis Moss, an ITC student, was field commander; Morris Dillard and James Felder, students at Morehouse and Clark, respectively, were co-chairs of the public relations committee; Ben Brown of Clark College was Treasurer of the organization and Danny Mitchell, also at Clark, was posted in the down-town area as senior intelligence officer; Julian Bond played an important role in communications. The members of the COAHR were King, Sullivan, Dillard, Robert Felder, James Felder, Carolyn Long, Mary Ann Smith Wilson, Ruby Doris Smith, A.D. King, Albert Brinson, Lenora Tate, Josephine Jackson, Lana Taylor, Frank Smith, Ben Brown, Danny Mitchell, Lydia Tucker, Leon Green, William Hickson, Johnny Parham, John Mack, Edmond Harper, Kenneth Crooks, John Bigson, J.A. Wilborn, and J.C. Harper. Charles Black was also a prominent member of the student movement. See Lincoln, "Strategy of a Sit-In," p. 22; Mays, *Born to Rebel*, p. 294; Neary, *Julian Bond: Black Rebel*, p. 51; Williams *The Bonds: An American Family*, p. 206.

CHAPTER THREE

1. *Atlanta Constitution*, 20 October 1960, pp. 1, 7. See also interview with Carolyn Long.

2. *Atlanta Constitution*, 21 October 1960, pp. 1, 12.

3. *Atlanta Constitution*, 22 October 1960, p. 1.

4. Lincoln, "Strategy of a Sit-In," p. 23.

5. Raines, *My Soul is Rested*, p. 89.

6. David L. Lewis, *King: A Critical Biography* (New York: Praeger Publishers, Inc., 1970), pp. 125-130; Raines, *My Soul is Rested*, pp. 93-94, 97-99.
7. *Atlanta Constitution*, 29 November 1960, p. 7; 30 November 1960, p. 11; 2 December 1960, p. 9.
8. Walker, *Protest and Negotiation*, p. 111; *Atlanta Inquirer*, 28 January 1961, p. 9.
9. *Atlanta Constitution*, 8 February 1961, p. 3.
10. *Ibid.*, 9 February 1961, p. 6.
11. *Ibid.*, 10 February 1961, p. 8.
12. *Ibid.*, 11 February 1961, p. 3.
13. *Atlanta Inquirer,* 14 January 1961, p. 2.
14. Walker, *Protest and Negotiation,* pp. 114, 118-19.
15. Raines, *My Soul is Rested,* p. 95.
16. *Atlanta Inquirer*, 11 March 1960, p. 1.
17. Interview with Alton Hornsby.
18. Walker, *Protest and Negotiation*, p. 124; See Raines, *My Soul is Rested*, for Lonnie King's comments on King's speech and Mays, *Born to Rebel*, p. 293.
19. Walker, *Protest and Negotiation*, pp. 124-125; *Atlanta Constitution*, 29 September 1961, p. l.
20. Interview with Mary Ann Smith Wilson.
21. Raines, *My Soul is Rested*, p. 96.

CHAPTER FOUR

1. Interview with Mary Ann Wilson.
2. Albert A. Thompson, "The Sit-In Technique: A Behavior Topology, *The Negro Education Review* 12 (April 1962): 36.
3. Interview with Lonnie King.
4. Interview with Dr. Lois Moreland, Spelman College, Atlanta, Georgia, 1 December 1979.
5. Interview with Dr. Benjamin E. Mays, 3316 Pamlico Drive, Atlanta, Georgia, 29 November 1978.
6. Interview with Wendell Whalum, Morehouse College, Atlanta, Georgia, 21 November 1978.
7. Interview with Dr. James Brawley, Clark College, Atlanta, Georgia, 24 April 1979.
8. Interviews with Julian Bond; Carolyn Long; Dr. Benjamin E. Mays; Dr. Lois Moreland; Dr. James Brawley.
9. Interview with Julian Bond.
10. Interview with Carolyn Long; *Atlanta Inquirer*, 24 October 1960, p. 1-A.
11. Walker, *Protest and Negotiation*, p. 113.
12. Interview with Lonnie King.
13. Interview with Alton Hornsby.
14. Interview with Dr. Benjamin E. Mays.
15. Interview with James P. Brawley.

16. Interview with Harry V. Richardson, Interdenominational Theological Center, Atlanta, Georgia 25 April 1979.
17. Interview with Dr. Margaret N. Rowley, Atlanta University, Atlanta, Georgia, 22 November 1978.
18. Interview with Mary Ann Smith Wilson.
19. Interview with Dr. Lois Moreland.
20. Interview with Dr. Clarence A. Bacote, Morehouse College, Atlanta, Georgia, 21 November 1978.
21. Lincoln, "Strategy of a Sit-In," p. 22; Walker, *Protest and Negotiation*, p. 21.
22. Interview with Lonnie King.
23. Interview with Julian Bond. Se also Williams, *The Bonds: An American Family*, pp. 208-09; Neary, *Julian Bond: Black Rebel*, pp. 62-64.
24. Interview with Lonnie King.
25. Interview with Julian Bond.
26. Interview with Carolyn Long.
27. Interview with Mary ann Smith Wilson.
28. Interview with Lonnie King.
29. Interview with Roswell F. Jackson, Morehouse College, Atlanta, Georgia, 17 April 1979.
30. Interview with Alton Hornsby.
31. Interview with Ralph Long, Sr., 1275 Fair Street, Atlanta, Georgia, 19 June 1979.
32. *Ibid.*
33. *Atlanta Inquirer*, 22 April 1961, p. 2; See interview with Carolyn Long for discussion of parental worrying over her well-being during demonstrations.
34. Leonard, "Second Battle of Atlanta," p. 45.
35. Interview with Julian Bond.
36. Neary, *Julian Bond: Black Rebel*, p. 55.
37. Williams, *The Bonds: An American Family*, p. 209.
38. Neary, *Julian Bond: Black Rebel*, p. 55.

CHAPTER FIVE

1. Interviews with Mays, Brawley, and Richardson.
2. Mays, *Born to Rebel*, p., 293.
3. Raines, *My Soul is Rested*, p. 87.
4. Interview with James P. Brawley.
5. *Ibid.*
6. Interview with Harry V. Richardson.
7. Interview with Julian Bond.
8. Lincoln, "Strategy of a Sit-In," p. 21.
9. Just what the presidents knew, and when they found it out is difficult to determine. Benjamin Mays says that "a committee of them [students] came to see me, February 17, 1960, to discuss their plans to begin sit-ins in downtown Atlanta on February 19." See Mays, *Born to Rebel*, pp. 287-290; Interview with

Mays. Jack Walker, in his study of the Atlanta student movement, writes that Mays persuaded students on February 17 to put their demonstrations off until after Martin Luther King, Jr.'s trial in adjoining DeKalb county for a traffic violation. See Walker, *Protest and Negotiation*, p. 72. In his book Mays acknowledges that he was concerned sit-ins might "affect adversely" King's trial. Mays goes on to say the council of Presidents met with "student government presidents from each of the six campuses and two students from each of the six campuses . . . for the first time," on February 20. Finally, Mays remembers students came to his house at midnight March 14 to tell him that the demonstrations were on for the next day.

10. Interview with Lonnie King.
11. *Ibid.*
12. Interview with Mary Ann Smith Wilson.
13. Interview with Julian Bond.
14. Interview with Lonnie King; Lewis, *King: A Critical Biography*, p. 114.
15. Raines, *My Soul is Rested*, pp. 86-87.
16. Interview with Mary Ann Smith Wilson.
17. Interview with Lonnie King.
18. Interview with Harry V. Richardson.
19. Interview with Julian Bond; Raines *My Soul is Rested*, p. 87.
20. Interview with Julian Bond.
21. Mays, *Born to Rebel*, p. 290.
22. Interview with Benjamin E. Mays.
23. Interview with Lonnie King.
24. *Ibid.*
25. *Ibid.*
26. Interview with Benjamin E. Mays.
27. Interview with James P. Brawley.
28. Albert Manley, "Charge to Students by Manley at Graduation," *Spelman Messenger*, August, 1960, p. 12.
29. Harry V. Richardson, "Some Religious Implications of the Sit-In Activities of American Students," *The Negro Education Review* 12 (April 1962); 51-54.
30. Interview with Lois Moreland.
31. *Ibid.*
32. *Ibid.*
33. Zinn, *Southern Mystique*, pp. 112-113; 132-134.
34. *Ibid.*, p. 136.
35. *Ibid.*, p. vii.
36. Interview with Wendell Whalum.
37. *Ibid.*
38. See footnote two in second chapter.
39. Interview with Wendell Whalum.
40. Helen Fuller, "We Are All So Very Happy, *New Republic*, April 25, 1960, pp. 14-15; Walker, *Protest and Negotiation*, p. 113; See also interviews with King and Bond.
41. Interview with Lonnie King.

42. Interview with Carolyn Long and Julian Bond; See p. 135 for discussion of newspaper.
43. *Atlanta Inquirer*, 11 March 1961, p. 2. See his other editorials from July 31, 1960 to March 25, 1961 in the *Inquirer*.
44. *Atlanta Constitution*, 25 March 1960, p. 10; George McMillan, "Sit Downs: The South's New Time Bomb," *Look*, 5 July 1960, p. 24; Interview with Lonnie King.
45. *Atlanta Journal*, 27 July 1960, p. 10; Tilman C. Cothran, "Socio-Psychological Aspects of the Sit-In Activities of American Students," *The Negro Education Review*, 12 (April 1960): 41-45.
46. Interview with Margaret Rowley.
47. Interview with Wendell Whalum and Lois Moreland.
48. Interview with Alton Hornsby.
49. Interview with Carolyn Long.
50. Arthur C. Banks, Jr., "Letters to the Editor," *Nation*, 17 September 1960, p. 140.
51. Interview with Alton Hornsby.
52. Interview with Lonnie King.
53. Interview with Lonnie King; Lois Moreland; see also interview with Mary Ann Smith Wilson; Howard Zinn, *The Southern Mystique*, p. 120.

Bibliography

Oral Interviews

Bacote, Clarence A. Morehouse College, Atlanta, Georgia. Interview, 21 November 1978.

Bond, Julian. Georgia State Capitol, Atlanta, Georgia. Interview, 10 April 1979.

Brawley, James P. Clark College, Atlanta, Georgia. Interview, 24 April 1979.

Hollowell, Donald L. 1389 Peachtree Street, Atlanta, Georgia. Interview, 30 November 1978.

Hornsby, Alton, Jr. Morehouse College, Atlanta, Georgia. Interview 3 May 1979.

Jackson, Roswell F. Morehouse College, Atlanta, Georgia. Interview, 17 April 1979.

King, Lonnie. Onyx Corporation, Atlanta, Georgia. Interview, 20 April 1979.

Long, Carolyn. 1275 Fair Street, Atlanta, Georgia. Interview, 13 June 1979.

Mays, Benjamin E. 3316 Pamlico Drive, Atlanta, Georgia. Interview, 29 November 1978.

Moreland, Lois. Spelman College, Atlanta, Georgia. Interview, 1 December 1978.

Richardson, Harry V. Interdenominational Theological Center, Atlanta, Georgia. Interview, 25 April 1979.

Rowley, Margaret N. Atlanta University, Atlanta, Georgia. Interview, 22 November 1978.

Whalum, Wendell. Morehouse College, Atlanta, Georgia. Interview, 21 November 1978.

Wilson, Mary Ann Smith. Southside Community Health Center, Atlanta, Georgia. Interview, 13 April 1979.

Primary Sources

Atlanta Constitution. March 1960—September 1961.

Atlanta Daily World. March 1960—September 1961.

Atlanta, Georgia. Atlanta University Special Collections. Sit-In Movement, Vertical File.

Atlanta, Georgia. Southern Regional Council. Newspaper Clipping Files.

Atlanta Inquirer. July 1960—September 1961.

Atlanta Journal. March 1960—September 1961.

Banks, Arthur C. "Letters to the Editor." *Nation*, 17 September, 1960, p. 140.

Manley, Albert. "Charge to Students by Manley at Graduation." *Spelman Messenger*, August, 1960, p. 12.

New York Times. March 1960—March 1961.

Pope, Roslyn and Wright, Marian. "Merrill Scholars Report." *Spelman Messenger*, November, 1959, pp. 5-6.

"Spelman College Students Receive Scholarships for Study and Travel." *Spelman Messenger*, May, 1959, p. 17.

Secondary Sources

Bennet, Lerone, Jr. *Confrontation: Black and White.* Baltimore: Penguin Books, 1966.

_____. "Plight of the Negro College Presidents." *Ebony,* October, 1960, pp. 138-144.

_____. "What Sit-Downs Mean to America." *Ebony*, June 1960, pp. 35-40.

Brisbane, Robert. *Black Activism: Racial Revolution in the United States, 1954-1970.* Valley Forge: Judson Press, 1974.

Bolster, Paul D. *Civil Rights Movements in Twentieth Century Georgia.* Ann Arbor: University Microfilms, 1972.

Bracey, John H.; Meier, August; and Rudwick, Elliott. *Conflict and Competition: Studies in the Recent Black Protest Movement.* Belmont, California: Wadsworth Publishing Company, Inc., 1971.

Cothran, Tilman C. "Some Socio-Psychological Implications of the 'Sit-In' Activities of American Students." *The Negro Education Review* 12 (April 1961): 41-45.

Farmer, James. *Freedom, When?.* New York: Random House, 1965.

Forman, James. *The Making of Black Revolutionaries: A Personal Account.* New York: MacMillan Company, 1972.

Fuller, Helen. "We Are All So Very Happy." *New Republic*, 25 April 1960, pp. 13-16.

Franklin, John Hope. *From Slavery to Freedom: A History of Negro Americans.* New York: Alfred A. Knopf, 1974.

Hoopes, James. *Oral History: An Introduction for Students.* Chapel Hill: University of North Carolina, 1979.

King, Martin Luther, Jr. "The Burning Truth in the South." *The Progressive*, May, 1960, pp. 8-10.

_____. *Stride Toward Freedom: The Montgomery Story.* New York: Harper and Row Publishers, 1964.

Leonard, George B. "The Second Battle of Atlanta." *Look*, 25 April 1961, pp. 31-42.

Lewis, David L. *King: A Critical Biography.* New York: Praeger Publishers, Inc., 1970.

Lincoln, C. Eric. "Strategy of a Sit-In." *The Reporter*, 5 January 1961, pp. 20-22.

Lomax, Louis E. *The Negro Revolt.* New York: Harper and Row Publishers, 1971.

_____. "The Negro Revolt Against the Negro Leaders." *Harper's Magazine*, June, 1960, pp. 41-48.

McMillan, George E. "Sit-Downs: The South's New Time Bomb." *Look*, 5 July 1960, pp. 21-25.

Machlin, Milton. *Atlanta.* New York: Avon Books, 1979.

Mays, Benjamin E. *Born to Rebel: An Autobiography.* New York: Charles Scribner's Sons, 1971.

_____. "A Plea for Straight Talk Between the Races." *The Atlantic Monthly*, December 1960, pp. 85-86.

Montell, William Lynwood. *The Saga of Coe Ridge: A Study in Oral History.* Knoxville: The University of Tennessee Press, 1970.

Neary, John. *Julian Bond: Black Rebel.* New York: William Morrow, 1971.

Peck, William, ed. *Sit-Ins: The Students Report.* New York: Congress of Racial Equality, 1960.

Raines, Howell. *My Soul is Rested: Movement Days in the Deep South.* New York: Bantam Books, 1978.

Richardson, Harry V. "Some Religious Implications of the 'Sit-In' Activities of American Students." *The Negro Education Review* 12 (April 1962): 51-54.

Sobel, Lester. *Civil Rights 1960-1966.* New York: Facts on File, 1967.

Southern Regional Council. *The Student Protest Movement.* Atlanta; SRC, Winter 1960.

_____. *The Student Protest Movement: A Recapitulation.* Atlanta: SRC., September 1961.

Thompson, Albert A. "The 'Sit-In' Technique: A Behavior Topology." *The Negro Education Review* 12 (April 1962): 36-39.

Tuskegee Institute, Division of Social Sciences. "The Tuskegee Institute Movement: A Sociological Analysis." May, 1960, (mimeographed).

Walker, Jack L. "The Functions of Disunity: Negro Leadership in a Southern City." In *Conflict and Competition: Studies in the Recent Black Protest Movement,* pp. 54-64. Edited by John H. Bracey, August Meier and Elliott Rudwick. Belmont, California: Wadsworth Publishing Company, 1971.

_____.*Protest and Negotiation: A Study of Negro Political Leaders in a Southern City.* Ann Arbor: University Microfilms, Inc., 1963.

Williams, Roger M. *The Bonds: An American Family.* New York: Atheneum, 1972.

Woodward, C. Vann. *The Strange Career of Jim Crow.* London: Oxford University Press, 1968.

Zinn, Howard, "Finishing School for Pickets." *Nation,* 6 August 1960, pp. 71-73.

_____. *SNCC: The New Abolitionists.* Boston: Beacon Press, 1968.

_____. *The Southern Mystique.* New York: Alfred A. Knopf, 1964.

An Appeal

For Human Rights

An Appeal
For Human Rights

We, the students of the six affiliated institutions forming the Atlanta University Center—Clark, Morehouse, Morris Brown, and Spelman Colleges, Atlanta University, and the Interdenominational Theological Center—have joined our hearts, minds, and bodies in the cause of gaining those rights which are inherently ours as members of the human race and as citizens of these United States.

We pledge our unqualified support to those students in this nation who have recently been engaged in the significant movement to secure certain long-awaited rights and privileges. This protest, like the bus boycott in Montgomery, has shocked many people throughout the world. Why? Because they had not quite realized the unanimity of spirit and purpose which motivated the thinking and action of the great majority of the Negro people. The students who instigate and participate in these sit-down protests are dissatisfied, not only with the existing conditions, but with the snail-like speed at which they are being ameliorated. Every normal human being wants to walk the earth with dignity and abhors any and all proscriptions placed upon him because of race or color. In essence, this is the meaning of the sit-down protests that are sweeping this nation today.

We do not intend to wait placidly for those rights which are already legally and morally ours to be meted out to us one at a time. Today's youth will not sit by submissively, while being denied all of the rights, privileges, and joys of life. We want to state clearly and unequivocally that we cannot tolerate, in a nation professing democracy and among people professing Christianity, the discriminatory conditions under which the Negro is living today in Atlanta, Georgia—supposedly one of the most progressive cities in the South.

Among the inequalities and injustices in Atlanta and in Georgia against which we protest, the following are outstanding examples:

(1) Education:

In the Public School System, facilities for Negroes and whites are separate and unequal. Double sessions continue in about half of the Negro Public Schools, and many Negro children travel ten miles a day in order to reach a school that will admit them.

On the university level, the state will pay a Negro to attend a school out of state rather than admit him to the University of Georgia, Georgia Tech, the Georgia Medical School, and other tax-supported public institutions.

According to a recent publication, in the fiscal year 1958 a total of $31,632,057.18 was spent in the State institutions of higher education for white only. In the Negro State Colleges only $2,001,177.06 was spent.

The publicly supported institutions of higher education are inter-racial now, except that they deny admission to Negro Americans.

(2) Jobs:

Negroes are denied employment in the majority of city, state, and federal governmental jobs, except in the most menial capacities.

(3) Housing:

While Negroes constitute 32% of the population of Atlanta, they are forced to live within 16% of the area of the city.

Statistics also show that the bulk of the Negro population is still:

a. locked into the more undesirable and overcrowded areas of the city;

b. paying a proportionally higher percentage of income for rental and purchase of generally lower quality property;

c. blocked by political and direct or indirect racial restrictions in its efforts to secure better housing.

(4) Voting:

Contrary to statements made in Congress recently by several Southern Senators, we know that in many counties in Georgia and other southern states, Negro college graduates are declared unqualified to vote and are not permitted to register.

(5) Hospitals:

Compared with facilities for other people in Atlanta and Georgia, those for Negroes are unequal and totally inadequate.

Reports show that Atlanta's 14 general hospitals and 9 related institutions provide some 4,000 beds. Except for some 430 beds at Grady Hospital, Negroes are limited to the 250 beds in three private Negro hospitals. Some of the hospitals barring Negroes were built with federal funds.

(6) Movies, Concerts, Restaurants:

Negroes are barred from most downtown movies and segregated in the rest.
Negroes must even sit in a segregated section of the Municipal Auditorium.
If a Negro is hungry, his hunger must wait until he comes to a "colored" restaurant, and even his thirst must await its quenching at a "colored" water fountain.

(7) Law Enforcement:

There are grave inequalities in the area of law enforcement. Too often, Negroes are maltreated by officers of the law. An insufficient number of Negroes is employed in the law-enforcing agencies. They are seldom if ever promoted. Of 830 policemen in Atlanta, only 35 are Negroes.

We have briefly mentioned only a few situations in which we are discriminated against. We have understated rather than overstated the problems. These social evils are seriously plaguing Georgia, the South, the nation, and the world.

We hold that;

(1) The practice of racial segregation is not in keeping with the ideals of Democracy and Christianity.

(2) Racial segregation is robbing not only the segregated but the segregator of his human dignity. Furthermore, the propagation of racial prejudice is unfair to the generations yet unborn.

(3) In times of war, the Negro has fought and died for his country; yet he still has not been accorded first-class citizenship.

(4) In spite of the fact that the Negro pays his share of taxes, he does not enjoy participation in city, county and state government at the level where laws are enacted.

(5) The social, economic, and political progress of Georgia is retarded by segregation and prejudices.

(6) America is fast losing the respect of other nations by the poor example which she sets in the area of race relations.

It is unfortunate that the Negro is being forced to fight, in any way, for what is due him and is freely accorded other Americans. It is unfortunate that even today some people should hold to the erroneous idea of racial superiority, despite the fact that the world is fast moving toward an integrated humanity.

The time has come for the people of Atlanta and Georgia to take a good look at what is really happening in this country, and to stop believing those who tell us that everything is fine and equal, and that the Negro is happy and satisfied.

It is to be regretted that there are those who still refuse to recognize the over-riding supremacy of the Federal Law.

Our churches which are ordained by God and claim to be the houses of all people, foster segregation of the races to the point of making Sunday the most segregated day of the week.

We, the students of the Atlanta University Center, are driven by past and present events to assert our feelings to the citizens of Atlanta and to the world.

We, therefore, call upon all people in authority—State, County, and City officials; all leaders in civic life—ministers, teachers, and business men; and all people of good will to assert themselves and abolish these injustices. We must say in all candor that we plan to use every legal and non-violent means at our disposal to secure full citizenship rights as members of this great Democracy of ours.

Willie Mays
President of Dormitory Council For the Students of Atlanta University

James Felder
President of Student Government Association
For the Students of Clark College

Marion D. Bennett
President of Student Association For the Students of
Interdenominational Theological Center

Don Clarke
President of Student Body For the Students of Morehouse College

Mary Ann Smith
Secretary of Student Government Association
For the Students of Morris Brown College

Roslyn Pope
President of Student Government Association For the
Students of Spelman College

Bibliographical
Information
and Acknowledgements

1. Meier, August and David Lewis. "History of the Negro Upper Class in Atlanta, Georgia, 1890-1958." *Journal of Negro Education* 28 (Spring 1959): 128-39. Published by permission of the *Journal of Negro Education*.

2. Walker, Jack L. "The Functions of Disunity: Negro Leadership in a Southern City." *Journal of Negro Education* 32 (Summer 1963): 227-36. Published by permission of the *Journal of Negro Education*.

3. Walker, Jack L. "Protest and Negotiation: A Case Study of Negro Leadership in Atlanta, Georgia." *Midwest Journal of Political Science* 7 (5/63): 99-124. Published by permission of the author.

4. Walker, Jack. L. *Sit-Ins in Atlanta*. New York: McGraw-Hill, 1964. Published by permission of the author.

5. Lincoln, C. Eric. "The Strategy of a Sit-In," *The Reporter*, Volume 24, January 5, 1961, pages 20-23. Published by permission of the author.

6. Newsom, Lionel and William Gorden. "A Stormy Rally in Atlanta," *Today's Speech*: 11 (4/63): 18-21. Published by permission of the Eastern Communication Association.

7. Fort, Vincent D. "The Atlanta Sit-In Movement, 1960-61: An Oral Study." M.A. thesis, Atlanta University, 1980. Published by permission of the author.

Index

Alexander, Cecil
  and secret Thanksgiving meeting, 80, 81
Allen, Ivan, Jr., ix, 87
  and race for mayor, 112
Allen, Robert, 101
American Dental Association
  Atlanta's black dentists excluded from, 61
American Medical Association
  Atlanta's black physicians excluded from, 61
An Appeal for Human Rights
  background of, 65, 157-158
  college presidents suggest, 133
  complete text, 183-187
  publication of, 19, 33
  quoted, 66, 90, 95-96, 105, 133
  reaction to, 66-67
A & P supermarket
  protests against, 71
Atlanta: A Second Look, 66, 133
  dramatizes discrimination, 65
Atlanta Chamber of Commerce, 83
Atlanta Committee for Cooperative Action, 36, 65, 70, 91
Atlanta Council for Cooperative Action, 133
Atlanta Daily World, 71, 135
  quoted, 72
  quoted on sit-ins, 68
Atlanta Inquirer, 76, 77, 85, 88, 98, 135, 142, 163
Atlanta Life Insurance Company, 6, 13
Atlanta Negro Voters League, 36, 91
Atlanta Student Defense Fund, 151

Bacote, Clarence A.
  quoted, 148/149
Banks, Arthur C., Jr.
  quoted opposing protests, 164
Barksdale, Marcellus, 169n5
Bearing the Cross (Garrow), viii
Bennet, Fred C., 172n44

Bennett, Marion D.
  signer of *Appeal*, 187
Bennette, Fred C. (*le Commandante*), 100
Bickers, Joseph T.
  quoted, 76
Bigson, John, 172n44
Black, Charles, 126, 172n44
Black Activism (Brisbane), 162
Black Muslims, 106
Blair, Ezell, 129
B'nai B'rith, 61
Boger, D. L.
  supports students, 164
Bond, Horace Mann, 153
Bond, Mrs. Horace Mann
  quoted, 153
Bond, Julian, 70, 131, 156, 161, 172n44
  and *Atlanta Inquirer*, 135
  helps write *Appeal*, 133
  quoted, 123, 124, 131, 147, 149-150, 159
  quoted on background of *Appeal*, 157-158
  quoted on giving up school work, 148/149
  quoted on his parents, 153
  quoted on instigation of protests, 129-130
Borders, William Holmes, 85, 103
  quoted on initial sit-ins, 69
Bracy, John
  his book *Conflict and Competition*, 119
Brawley, James, 155, 159
  quoted, 146, 148, 155-156, 160
Brazeal, Brailsford, 146
Brinson, Albert, 172n44
Brisbane, Robert
  his book *Black Activism*, 162
  involvement in the movement, 162
Brown, Benjamin, 81, 85, 100, 172n44
  quoted, 73
  his speech at 3/10/61 meeting quoted, 89, 107, 109

Brown, Ernest, 101, 139
Brown, Lee
  quoted, 153

Carson, Clayborne
  his book *In Struggle*, viii
Cayton, Horace, 4, 14
Chafe, William
  his book *Civilities and Civil Rights*, vii
Chautauqua Circle, 7, 9, 10, 11, 12, 13
Citizens' Trust Company, 6, 7, 13
Civilities and Civil Rights (Chafe), vii
Civil Rights Bill of 1957, 63
Clarke, Don
  signer of *Appeal*, 187
Clement, Rufus B. 132, 155
  and 3/9/60 meeting, 67
  proposes *Appeal*, 157
  quoted, 157
  quoted on *Appeal*, 65
  quoted on initial sit-ins, 69
Cochrane, Warren, 76, 91
Colonial Stores, Inc.
  protests against, 77, 98
Committee on an Appeal for Human Rights,
  36/37, 74, 91/92, 98, 100, 131
  creation of, 69, 97
*Conflict and Competition: Studies in the
  Recent Black Protest Movement* (Bracy,
  Meier, Rudwick), 119
Cothran, Tilman C.
  supports students, 163
Crooks, Kenneth, 172n44
Cross, Lonnie, 131, 132
Cunningham, James, 155

Dillard, Morris J., 100, 172n44
  helps write *Appeal*, 133
Drake, St. Clair, 4, 14
Dunbar, Leslie
  quoted, 17-18

Eckford, Elizabeth, 124
Eisenhower, Dwight David, 62
Emory, Elroy, 102
Empire Real Estate Board, 76

Felder, James, 100, 172n44
  signer of *Appeal*, 187
Felder, Robert ("Tex"), 100, 101, 172n44
Forman, James
  quoted, 124
Fort, Vincent, x

Garrow, David J.
  his book *Bearing the Cross*, viii
Georgia Real Estate Loan and Trust
  Company, 6, 11
Gibson, James, 70
Gorden, William, x
Green, Leon, 172n44
GUTS (Georgians Unwilling to Surrender),
  82

Harper, Edmond, 172n44
Harper, J. C., 172n44
Hartsfield, William B. (mayor of Atlanta),
  viii, ix, 78, 159
  and 3/9/60 meeting, 67
  asks for extension of truce, 79-80
  quoted, 82, 86, 88
  quoted on *Appeal*, 66-67, 95-96
  quoted on *Brown* commemoration march,
  72
  quoted on school bombing, 83
  speech to the Hungry Club, 70
  and thirty-day truce, 139-140
Herndon, Alonzo F.
  founder of Atlanta Life Insurance
  Company, 6
Hickson, William, 172n44
Hill, Jessie, 70, 81, 85
Hollowell, Donald L., 68-69
  counsel for many students, 133
Holman, M. Carl, 70, 85
  and *Atlanta Inquirer*, 135
  involvement in movement, 163
  quoted, 88
Hornsby, Alton
  on his mother's attitude toward protests,
  151
  quoted, 130, 132
  quoted on 3/10/61 meeting, 141
  quoted on faculty involvement with
  movement, 164

quoted on his professors' attitudes toward protests, 164
Hungry Club
speech to by Mayor Hartsfield, 70

Inquirers (literary club), 13
In Struggle (Carson), viii

Jackson, Josephine, 172n44
Jackson, Roswell F.
quoted on his daughter's participation, 151
Jenkins, Herbert (Atlanta Chief of Police), 73, 159, 160
Johnson, Leroy, 70, 85
Junior Chamber of Commerce, 83
Junior Matrons, 9

Kennedy, John F., ix, 136
phone call to Coretta Scott King, 93n3, 140
Kennedy, Robert
calls judge in Martin Luther King, Jr.'s case, 140
Killian, Lewis M.
study (with C. U. Smith) of Tallahassee protests, 17-18, 24
King, A. D., 136, 172n44
King, Coretta Scott
John Kennedy's phone call to, 93n3, 140
King, Lonnie C., 70, 71, 73, 81, 84, 85, 88, 100, 129, 131, 161, 172n44
and 3/9/60 meeting, 67
accepts settlement, 87
arrested, 78
and *Atlanta Inquirer*, 135
and *Brown* commemoration march, 134
Chairman of the Committee on an Appeal for Human Rights, 69
helps write *Appeal*, 133
initially reluctant to accept agreement, 141
his initial response to sit-in movement, 63-64
married with family, 148/149
meeting with Richard Rich (6/24/60), 75-76

and plan to effect 1960 presidential election, 135-136, 140
quoted, 125, 131-132, 135-136, 135-136, 141, 143, 145-146, 147, 148/149, 158
quoted on background of *Appeal*, 158
quoted on *Brown* commemorative march, 159-160
quoted on faculty involvement with movement, 164, 165
quoted on instigation of protests, 130
quoted on meeting with college presidents, 157
quoted on summer activities, 135
and secret Thanksgiving meeting, 80
King, Martin Luther, Jr., viii, vii, ix, 31, 49, 64
and 3/10/61 meeting, 141
his arrest, 99, 139
arrested, 78
his arrest planned to effect 1960 presidential race, 136
persuaded to join protests, 78, 136
quoted, 121
released from jail, 78
and secret Thanksgiving meeting, 80
his sentence, 140
speaks at 2/15/61 meeting, 84
speech at 3/10/61 meeting, ix-x, 89-90, 109-111, 142
King, Martin Luther, Sr.
quoted, 91/92
and 3/10/61 meeting, 141
his speech at 3/10/61 meeting quoted, 108
supports John Kennedy for president, 140
Knoxville, Tennessee
sit-ins there, 25-26, 54
Ku Klux Klan, 82, 86, 99, 102-103

Lee, Bernard, 136
Lee, Gwendolyn, 102
Lewis, David, x, viii
Lincoln, C. Eric, x
Links, 9
Long, Carolyn, 172n44
helps write *Appeal*, 133
quoted, 127, 130-131, 147, 150, 164
Long, Ralph
his involvement in protests, 151-152
Long, Mrs. Ralph

on protests, 152

McCain, Franklin, 129
Mack, John, 172n44
McNeil, Joseph, 129
Maddox, Lester
  and race for mayor, 112
Manley, Albert, 155
  quoted, 161
Manley, Alvin E.
  proposes drafting *Appeal*, 65
Mays, Benjamin E., 134, 155, 159
  on *Brown* commemorative march, 159
  persuades students to postpone initial
    demonstrations, 64
  quoted, 72, 131, 146, 147-148, 155, 159,
    160, 174n9
  and secret Thanksgiving meeting, 80
Mays, Willie
  signer of *Appeal*, 187
Meier, August, viii, x
  his book *Conflict and Competition*, 119
Merrill Scholarship Program, 125, 170n9
Mitchell, Daniel, 100, 172n44
Moreland, Lois, 165
  quoted, 146, 148, 164
  quoted on her role in movement, 161
Moss, Otis, 100, 101, 172n44
Mutual Federal Savings and Loan
  Association, 7, 13
Myrdal, Gunnar
  quoted, 35-36

NAACP, 36/37, 61, 69, 72, 91, 107
National Fuel Corporation, 6
National Students Association, 61
National Urban League, 61
Newsom, Lionel, x
  supports students, 163
Nixon, Richard, 136
Norrell, Robert J
  his book *Reaping the Whirlwind*, vii

Parham, Johnny, 172n44
Patrick, Clarence H.
  quoted on Winston-Salem, N. C. sit-ins,
    26, 55
Perry, Hemon

his varied businesses listed, 6
Pierce, Joe, 131, 148/149
Pope, Roslyn, 125
  helps write *Appeal*, 133
  signer of *Appeal*, 187
Proudfoot, Merrill
  quoted on Knoxville, Tennessee sit-ins,
    25-26, 54

Reaping the Whirlwind (Norrell), vii
Retail Merchants Association, 83
Rich, Richard H., ix
  described, 75
  meeting with student leaders (6/24/60),
    75-76
  and secret Thanksgiving meeting, 80-81
Richardson, Harry V., 155
  his article on movement, 161
  quoted, 148, 156, 158-159
Richmond, David, 129
Rich's, Inc.
  described, 75
  protests against, 76, 77, 96
  their attempts to end protests, 79
Rowley, Margaret
  quoted, 148, 163
Rudwick, Elliott
  his book *Conflict and Competition*, 119

SCLC, 61
Scott, C. A., 74, 76
  attempts to arrange meetings, 71
  quoted, 68
Service Company, 6
Service Engineering and Construction
  Company, 6
Service Pharmacies, 6
Service Realty Company, 6
Sigma Pi Phi (Boule of), 7-8
Smith, Charles U.
  study (with Lewis M. Killian) of
    Tallahassee protests, 17-18
Smith, Frank, 172n44
Smith, Ruby Doris, 124, 148/149, 150,
    172n44
  quoted, 133
SNCC, viii, 61
Southern Christian Leadership Conference
  (*See* SCLC)

Southern Christian Leadership Council, 36
Southern Manifesto, 62
The Southern Mystique (Zinn), 162
Southern Regional Council, 61
Standard Life Insurance Company, 6
Student-Adult Liaison Committee, 74, 78,
    83, 91/92, 98, 106, 140, 156
  creation of, 73
  and secret Thanksgiving meeting, 80
Student Nonviolent Coordinating Committee
    (*See* SNCC)
Sullivan, Herschelle, 81, 86, 88, 100, 125,
    172n44
  accepts settlement, 87
  helps write *Appeal*, 133
  initially reluctant to accept agreement,
    141
  and plan to effect 1960 presidential
    election, 135-136, 140

Tait, Lenora, 102
Tate, Lenora, 172n44
Taylor, Lana, 172n44
Troutman, Robert, Sr., ix, 86-87, 140
Tucker, Lydia, 172n44
The Twelve, 7, 9, 11, 13
Twenty-Seven Club, 7-8

Urban League, 91

Vandiver, Ernest (Governor of Georgia), 72,
    73
  and *Brown* commemoration march, 134
  quoted on *Appeal*, 67, 95-96

Walden, A. T., viii, ix, 68-69, 85, 140
  background of, 85
  quoted, 86
  speech at 3/10/61 meeting quoted, 89,
    107
Walker, Jack, x
Westside Voters League, 36
Whalum, Wendell
  involvement in the movement, 162
  quoted, 146, 163-164
White Citizens Councils, 62
Wilborn, J. A., 172n44
Wilburn, Harold

denounces settlement at 3/10/61 meeting,
    89, 108
Williams, Samuel
  involvement in the movement, 162-163
  quoted, 73, 84
Wilson, James Q.
  quoted, 24, 41, 53
Wilson, Mary Ann Smith, 133, 172n44
  quoted, 126, 130, 135, 142, 145, 148,
    157, 158
  quoted on the support of her parents, 150
  signer of *Appeal*, 187
Winston-Salem, North Carolina
  sit-ins there, 26, 55
Wright, Marian
  quoted, 125

Yates and Milton Drug Stores, 7
Young, Whitney
  supports students, 163

Zinn, Howard, 164
  his book *The Southern Mystique*, 162
  his involvement in the movement, 161-
    162

TITLES IN THE SERIES

Martin Luther King, Jr.
and the
Civil Rights Movement

DAVID J. GARROW, EDITOR

1-3. *Martin Luther King, Jr.: Civil Rights Leader, Theologian, Orator*, Edited by David J. Garrow

4-6. *We Shall Overcome: The Civil Rights Movement in the United States in the 1950s and 1960s*, Edited by David J. Garrow

7. *The Walking City: The Montgomery Bus Boycott, 1955-1956*, edited by David J. Garrow

8. *Birmingham, Alabama, 1956-1963: The Black Struggle for Civil Rights*, Edited by David J. Garrow

9. *Atlanta, Georgia, 1960-1961: Sit-Ins and Student Activism*, Edited by David J. Garrow

10. *St. Augustine, Florida, 1963-1964: Mass Protest and Racial Violence*, Edited by David J. Garrow

11. *Chicago 1966: Open-Housing Marches, Summit Negotiations and Operation Breadbasket*, Edited by David J. Garrow

12. *At the River I Stand: Memphis, the 1968 Strike, and Martin Luther King*, by Joan Turner Beifuss

13. *The Highlander Folk School: A History of its Major Programs, 1932-1961*, by Aimee Isgrig Horton

14. *Conscience of a Troubled South: The Southern Conference Educational Fund, 1946-1966*, by Irwin Klibaner

15. *Direct Action and Desegregation, 1960-1962: Toward a Theory of the Rationalization of Protest*, by James H. Laue

16. *The Sit-In Movement of 1960*, by Martin Oppenheimer

17. *The Student Nonviolent Coordinating Committee: The Growth of Radicalism in a Civil Rights Organization*, by Emily Stoper

18. *The Social Vision of Martin Luther King, Jr.*, by Ira G. Zepp, Jr.